A MASTER SPEAKS

Volume Two

Articles from *Share International* magazine

SHARE INTERNATIONAL FOUNDATION

Amsterdam • London

Published by Share International Foundation
PO Box 41877, 1009 DB, Amsterdam, the Netherlands
All rights reserved
Copyright: © 2017 Benjamin Creme Estate
ISBN/EAN: 978-94-91732-11-9

Manufactured in the United States of America on
recycled paper

First edition, April 2017

*The cover picture is reproduced from a painting by
Benjamin Creme:* **Open Mandala***, 1972. Floating in space,
the Open Mandala presents to the viewer a void which
attracts and holds the attention in the Void of Cosmos.
With the attention held there at the centre of the picture,
the Void draws forth the aspiration and longing of the
viewer for unity with all things. In response, the Void
releases its energy to stimulate and renew the viewer's
aspiration and desire for union.*

In loving memory of Benjamin Creme
and with gratitude to his Master

Contents

Preface to Volume One

In every age, major and lesser spiritual teachers have guided humanity. We know them, among others, as Hercules, Hermes, Rama, Mithra, Vyasa, Sankaracharya, Krishna, Buddha, the Christ and Mohammed. They are the custodians of a Plan for the evolution of humanity and the other kingdoms of nature. This Plan works out through the agency of the esoteric Hierarchy of Masters of the Wisdom.

The Masters are those members of the human family who have made the evolutionary journey ahead of us; who, having perfected Themselves — by the same steps by which we advance — have accepted the responsibility of guiding the rest of us to that same achievement. They have stood behind the whole evolutionary process, guiding and helping us, through a gradual expansion of consciousness, to become, like Them, perfected and illumined.

The majority of the Masters live in the remote mountain and desert areas of the world, contacting the world but seldom, and doing Their work through Their disciples, mainly by telepathic communication. It is through this means that I have the privilege of being in contact with one of the Masters. For various reasons His identity may not be revealed for the time being, but I may say that He is one of the senior members of the Hierarchy, Whose name is well known to esotericists in the West.

His information, training and stimulus have enabled me to do the work I am engaged in: making known that Maitreya, the Christ, the Supreme Head of the Hierarchy of Masters, is in the world. He has been in London since July 1977. There He lives and works as a modern man, concerned with modern problems – political, economic and social. He is a spiritual but not a religious teacher, an educator in the broadest sense of the word, showing the way out of the present world crisis.

One of the means by which my co-workers and I spread this information is the monthly magazine *Share International*. Since its beginning, in January 1982, my Master has been kind enough to write an article for every issue, and, as far as I know, this makes *Share International* the only magazine in the world to number one of the Masters among its contributors.

The articles contain a wealth of wisdom, insight and information. In one of the articles, my Master explains His purpose in writing these articles (May 1992).

"It has been My endeavour, over the years, to present to the readers of this magazine a picture of the life ahead, to inspire a happy and positive approach to that future and to equip them with the tools of knowledge to deal correctly with the problems which daily arise upon the way. From My vantage point of experience and insight, I have sought to act as 'look-out' and guard, to warn of approaching danger, and to enable you, the reader, to act with courage and conviction in service to the Plan.

"For many, this has not been a task performed in vain; many have found in My words both inspiration and guidance. Many await, avidly, their monthly libation of truth. Others read calmly, with a distant eye and even more distant mind and heart, while others again are baffled and know not what to think."

We have now collected all of the Master's articles in one volume from the first issue of the magazine in January 1982 to December 2003, under the title *A Master Speaks*. This is to present the wealth of wisdom to the readers at large. I hope that you will find His words inspiring and relevant. My Master's name will be known after Maitreya the Christ has come to the fore and has made His public appeal to humanity – an event which we believe is now near.

Benjamin Creme, March 2004

Editor's note to Volume Two

This book, *A Master Speaks, Volume Two*, contains articles dictated by Benjamin Creme's Master and published in *Share International* magazine from January 2004 to December 2016. It has been long in the making and was planned with Benjamin Creme's co-operation and approval. Sadly, he died in October 2016, some months before it was completed. This book is now published in his memory and can be seen as a valedictory volume, marking the ending of Benjamin Creme's lifetime's work with his Master. The legacy of this work lives on in the new volume – a product of their close relationship.

A brief explanation of the process involved in receiving the articles may be of interest. Benjamin Creme's Master dictated the articles telepathically through a process of mental overshadowing, but it required of Benjamin Creme – as the recipient of the articles – the ability to hold his attention on the Buddhic plane, the level of spiritual intuition. Judging by his descriptions, receiving these articles required considerable sustained concentration. Sometimes the process seemed to flow easily while at other times it appeared, from the point of view of an observer, to take more energy and effort.

Readers will notice that the articles gradually became shorter and that in some months no new article was given. This was the case in 2015 and 2016 and was due to Benjamin Creme's declining health. He was then already in his 90s. It was a service he gladly undertook, and he managed to gather enough strength to convey a final brief and inspiring statement from his Master only 19 days before he died.

As an **Addendum** to the Master's articles, we have included Messages from Maitreya communicated through Benjamin Creme during his interviews between 2000 and 2010.

From October 2007 *Share International* began printing the date the article was dictated by Benjamin Creme's Master. Therefore two dates are printed at the end of each article.

The Masters' pledge

As the dark clouds of war gather and obscure the sunlit sky of peace, the response of humanity is twofold: mute acceptance and compliance with the will of the warmongers, or active and spirited resistance to their plans and ploys. Today, we see both reactions in equal measure. Half the world is caught up in the glamour of 'a war against terrorism' (without recognizing the underlying cause) and in terrorism itself. The other half deplores both terrorism and the lack of understanding of its genesis. They know that changes, on a major scale, alone hold the key to ending this atrocious evil, and call to the leaders of nations to recognize and address the inequalities which so unfairly divide the world.

This latter group must grow and increase their resistance to the plans of those, now in power, who so threaten the stability of the world. They must find each other and work together, knowing that they work and speak for the vast but silent majority who share their longing for peace and manifested justice.

Peace will only come when justice reigns, when sharing has opened men's hearts and awakened them to trust. Thus men must work and speak loudly for justice and sharing which alone will bring an end to men's suffering, to terrorism and war. We, your Elder Brothers, are ready to do Our part. We will potentize all actions taken on behalf of the Common Good. We await the opportunity to manifest Our strength; to help to right the wrongs of the past; to show men the uselessness of war. We pledge our support of all who call for an end to war, for the restoration of sanity and balance in the affairs of men, for the creation of justice and freedom for all.

Help Us to help you. Help Us to do Our part. We long to act, as always, in the interest of the Common Good, which, in Our understanding, is the best interests of all men. Thus it is that We advocate sharing; thus do We advise justice; thus do We see freedom and peace as the culmination of sharing and justice.

Let us work together for the rescue of this world. Let us abandon differences in the interests of the race. Let sanity triumph and bring men to see their mutual need for peace, and the restoration of an ailing world.

Many await the future in dread, fearful that man has lost his way, that it is now too late to find the path to peace. We counsel otherwise. We know that the path to peace is simply found, needing only the creation of justice and trust. We know that sharing alone will engender that trust, and bring men to abandon both terrorism and war. Thus will it be, and thus will men respond to Maitreya's message of Brotherhood and Justice, free at last from the glamours of fear and mistrust, ready to create the future in deed and in joy.

January/February 2004

A new serenity

It will not be long before the world realizes that something quite extraordinary is taking place. Already, signs are appearing that many people are becoming aware of a new atmosphere, a new turn of thought, difficult to place or describe, which gives them hope and alleviates the stress of the recent past. Something, intangible but strongly present, is making itself felt on a wide scale.

Those who know, of course, of the presence of Maitreya and His Group, have for long experienced this feeling of comfort and quiet joy, this confident assurance that all will be well, no matter the circumstances of the day. In growing numbers, now, this sense of security and ultimate good amid the chaos and challenges of the present, is strengthening. Slowly and surely, people are awakening to the presence of they know not what, but dimly sense that it is for the good and safety of all.

Thus does the Great Lord ease the pain of the present conditions and prepare the multitudes to respond to His words. Thus does He ensure their understanding of the priorities of the complex international situation which threatens the well-being of all.

Many will be amazed by their unusual calm and objectivity in conditions of stress. Many more will wonder at their ready tolerance of long-standing opponents and rivals. Thus the Great Lord works to mitigate the suffering of so many.

In time, men will associate their new-found ease with the One Who speaks so simply of trust, of sharing and peace. They will recognize that the simplicity belies a profound understanding of the human condition and the needs of all. So encouraged, they will follow His advocacy and raise their voices in response. Thus will the Voice of the People grow in strength and purpose and, echoing round the world, will call loudly to the leaders for sanity, justice and peace. Then will the men of power begin to realize that their day is over, that the people understand and demand their God-given right to health and happiness, freedom and justice, trust and blessed peace.

Thus will it be, and thus will the peoples of Earth call for the Great Lord to speak directly to all, to cement their growing unity, and to indicate the steps to transformation of the world. Then will Maitreya reveal His true identity and nature. The Day of Declaration will be for humanity a new beginning, and will inspire from men, as never before, the best that is in them.

March 2004

The ultimate triumph

When a nation comes to adulthood, to maturity, it relates to other nations in a completely different way than hitherto. It begins to respect the Rule of Law, which binds all nations together in mutual responsibility and need. The sign of a growing maturity is precisely this respect for the laws which men have found necessary to living together in peace.

From time to time, a nation may feel powerful enough to ignore the law which irks its ambition to dominate, and to make war despite the warnings of restraint from its friends.

Thus it is today that the United States, now, alone, a 'superpower', vexes and worries the people of more mature nations who have grown to see the folly of unilateral action outside the Rule of Law.

The young and over-confident 'superpower', flexing its muscles, will overreach itself, and the sooner this happens the safer for the world. Already a steadily growing chaos exacts due cost in loss of life, both American and Iraqi. The seal of Pandora's Box has been broken and from it has stepped a monster, out of control. To be sure, the US administration wear as brave a face as they can muster, but behind the scenes, they are worried indeed, and seek desperately a less than ignominious method of withdrawal.

Meanwhile, the defeated Iraqi army fights a guerrilla war with some success, while religious groups, seizing their opportunity, increase the tension with calls for civil war. Thus, the paramount adventure of the American President, designed to demonstrate the invincibility of the United States, has little to show for its efforts and very much still to lose.

When, at last, the US Government sees for itself the folly of this reckless and unnecessary war, it will not, of course, admit this to the world. Rather, it will seek to gain the support of the United Nations to extricate itself from this embarrassing blunder, and, if possible, to lay the blame elsewhere.

When, among nations, the Rule of Law is ignored, the whole world suffers. Thus, today, the tension which has accompanied this futile demonstration of military strength affects millions, innocent of all terrorist action or mayhem. The world is struggling now with epidemics of all kinds as the human immune system breaks down under the stress. Did the warmongers but realize the karmic effects of their ill-considered actions, they might well make amends and take sightings for another course.

Maitreya, meanwhile, watches carefully this inharmonious situation, ready to intervene if necessary, ready to emerge when possible. Remember that Maitreya is in no doubt about the ultimate triumph of those who stand behind Him, who value peace and justice, freedom and love. He knows that these are the mainsprings of human existence and comes to see them enthroned in all.

April 2004

The Path to the Sun

It is often to be observed that people do not always believe the evidence of their own eyes. Hence the rejection of many experiences which would have been valuable to them as they search for meaning and purpose in their lives. It is common, for example, that many disbelieve that they have seen a UFO, as they are generally known, when all evidence shows otherwise. People are loath to embrace the new and unknown, however much to do so it might be to their benefit. In this way, they inhibit their awareness and growth.

For many years now, the craft emerging from our sister planets have roamed our skies, done immeasurable service on our behalf, and, from time to time, given ample and inspiring evidence of their reality and presence. In ones and twos and untold numbers, they have worked selflessly to mitigate, within the karmic Law, the harmful results of our foolishness and ignorance. Many on Earth have seen them, have stood in awe and wonder at their obvious mastery of space, and, fearful of ridicule, kept silence. Thus the knowledge of their reality and the grateful understanding of their purpose has been lost to men. Why should this be so? Why should men reject that which is most to their betterment to accept and understand?

There are several reasons why men behave so unreasonably in this way. Chief among them is fear. The great numbing fear of possible destruction lies deep within the human psyche, ready to rise and condition all reactions, all spontaneous gestures of hope and wonder. It has, alas, always been so for many.

The governments and the media of most countries have failed in their duty to educate and enlighten the masses. Much is known by many governmental agencies and withheld from the public. Above all, the *harmlessness* of the UFO, even when known, is never affirmed. On the contrary, everything concerning them, while wrapped in vague mystery, is presented as threat.

People in positions of power and control know that if their people knew the true nature of the UFO phenomenon, and understood them to be envoys from civilizations far ahead of ours, they would no longer accept, passive and mute, the conditions of life on Earth. They would demand that their leaders invite these aerial guests to land openly, and to teach us how to live and achieve in the same fashion.

The time is not far off when this will be the case. The time is coming when the true nature of life on planets other than Earth will be common knowledge; when men will begin to think of the Solar System as an interrelated whole, the planets at various points in evolution, but all working together to fulfil the Plan of the Solar Logos, and to help and sustain each other on the way.

May 2004

The ultimate choice

When mankind sees, at last, the folly of its present fascination with violence and war, and discards the means to carry out its acts of violence, it will undergo a remarkable transformation. The first signs of this most welcome change in human behaviour can be seen in the millions who now march denouncing war and calling for justice and peace. These demonstrations, spontaneous and worldwide, are a sure indication that mankind is ready to renounce the past, and, when properly led, to change direction. This time is fast approaching.

Amid the trauma and stressful conditions of the present, a new vision of the future is presenting itself to the hearts and minds of millions who, to a greater or lesser degree, respond. Men are awakening to the necessity of peace if mankind is to survive. Few there are who doubt this in their hearts, however much they may be embroiled in war. The stage thus is set for the ultimate choice before mankind.

To the average onlooker, the world is torn and dominated by those who do not share the vision of peace, who see only opportunities for wealth and power in every conflagration. While these are many, the majority of men are tired of the uselessness of war, and seek strategies to put an end to such folly for ever. In their hearts burns the hope of a new time of peace and progress for all. These people, in every country, represent the hope of the world.

It is to them that Maitreya will address Himself on His emergence. It is to them that He presents the vision of the future, even now. They, in their many millions, will quickly respond to His advocacy, and set alight the hope of all.

Thus will Maitreya persuade men that further reckless strife is useless and dangerous. That the problems of today are global and cannot be solved by war. That co-operation alone will bring men peace and plenty. That only as brothers, hand in hand, can they enter the new world which awaits their care.

Thus will men decide, and turn back from the abyss. Thus will they demonstrate their choice for life and happiness, and, eyes alight with hope, begin together the task of reconstructing this world.

The time of decision is nigh, almost upon us. Maitreya is ready, eager to show the way, point the new direction. Millions await His counsel and inspiration, wisdom and love. Maitreya will vouchsafe the future for all.

June 2004

The Teachers and the taught

Many are the times, throughout his long history, when man has lost his way, but never, until now, has he strayed so far from his destined path. Never, before, has he been in such need of succour, and never, until now, has that help been so readily available. For long ages, the Law has restricted the measure of aid which might be given; man's free will is sacrosanct and may not be infringed. Today, for the first time in countless centuries, more aid can be freely given than ever before. Today, at his moment of greatest need and despair, the bountiful hands of his Elder Brothers can open, and provide the succour he longs for.

All that is required is the request from man himself. All that is needed is the readiness to accept the advice and wisdom of the Brotherhood, and to change direction.

Many at this time of crisis have lost hope and wait fearfully for the end of all. They know nothing of the hope which fills their future and languish in the midst of change. Many more are impatient with the present and seek change at any cost. They feel the future beckoning with they know not what, and champ at the bit in their eagerness to experience the new. All are subject to the influence of the tensions and stress which characterize this time of change, and, in the light of their disposition, react accordingly.

Into this complex situation the Masters make Their approach. They must so act that man's free will is not transgressed, yet seek to help in every way the Law allows. Fine will be the judgement needed in many circumstances and cases until a modus-operandi is evolved acceptable to all.

We, your Elder Brothers, counsel the democratic process, with full participation, as that which brings freedom and justice to each one. Nevertheless, there will be many times when Our age-long experience and vantage point in evolution will be to man's advantage and betterment to accept.

Thus shall we work together, the Teachers and the taught, in harmony and trust; and thus will man learn the ways of the past, of his forefathers, and so bring his aspiration into line with his preordained purpose.

Thus will it be, and thus will man begin to realize the essentials of life, and begin to discard the multitude of useless attachments which today distort his vision, create his unhappiness and threaten his very existence.

Soon, Maitreya, the Master of the Masters, will begin His open mission. Soon, men will be able to hear His teachings and assess them for themselves. Many will find in them the Truth so simply evident that they will quickly join His band of warriors and share His burden. May all who read these words be among them.

July/August 2004

The forward path

Preparatory to every shift in human consciousness there is a pause, a moment of stillness, in which the achievements of the past are reappraised and, if found wanting, discarded. Thus it is today as man assesses what is relevant and needful to preserve for future use, and what is dispensable in the light of his growing awareness and insight. Left to himself, this period for man would be long indeed. Many are the experiments which he would require to make, and many are the possibilities of error which could occur, ere the right path was found and the right steps taken.

From now on, man can avail himself, if he so chooses, of the help and experience of Us, his Elder Brothers, Who stand ready to aid and inspire when called upon to do so.

Thus is this a time without precedent, when the Helpers are at hand in every situation, careful to maintain man's divine free will, but eagerly willing to give of Their age-long wisdom and hard-fought-for experience and knowledge.

Much that today seems important will pass away, to be replaced by simpler and more natural ways of living and relationship. Gone, you may be sure, will be the blasphemy of millions dying needlessly of want in the midst of overflowing plenty. Gone, too, will be the intolerance which so disfigures the human spirit today. Gone, for ever, the urge to dominate, subdue and exploit the resources and territory of smaller and weaker nations. In their place will grow a new realism, an understanding of the inter-connectedness of all men and of their mutual rights and obligations. Men and nations will seek to live by the rule of law and the requirements of peace and security for all men.

Soon, the beginning of such a process will make its appearance. Already, the men whose eyes are attuned to the future are making known their insights and gaining attention. More and more, many will turn to them for assurance and guidance, and in this way the new thought will take root. Gradually, a transformation will take place in human thinking and, inevitably, the old will give way to a new and saner approach to the problems of life.

Thus, in a fiery cauldron, the shape of the future is being fashioned now. The outlines, as yet, are dim and indistinct, yet sufficiently clear, to those whose eyes are keen, to give assurance and hope that man is awakening to his true identity and purpose, and, despite the vicissitudes of the time, well set on his forward path.

September 2004

A call for sanity

The citizens of the United States of America are approaching a time of critical decision. On their decision, in November, this year, may depend the future happiness of many millions, not alone American, but of many other countries. One would have thought that this decision would not be difficult to make, that the choice was surely obvious to all who treasure peace and right relationship.

However, it appears that there are those who think otherwise, who reserve for themselves the right to invade other countries on the pretext that they might be plotting harm for them. Such pre-emptive action, one would have assumed, was long ago abandoned by modern, civilized states, and relegated to man's illegal past.

Not so, sadly, we are assured. The present American administration, far from showing remorse for their unjust and cruel invasion of Iraq, proudly assert, if re-elected, their firm resolve to continue their programme of pillage in their 'war on terror'.

To fight a 'war on terror' is to fight a phantom, a useless, costly and dangerous exercise. Terror is the Hydra, a many-headed monster: each head severed, as Hercules discovered, is replaced by two. This US administration, in its arrogance and ignorance, has fallen blindly into the trap. Those who suffer are the American people, their victims, and the world as a whole.

There is but one way to deal with terror, to end, forever, this canker in our midst: to seek its cause.

There are, of course, several causes of terrorism, but above all in importance is the unbalanced distribution of the world's resources. This creates the dangerous gulf between the nations which drives men to use terror to realize their dreams. They are desperate men, who feel they have nothing to lose. There is an immense, untapped army of such desperate people ready to die, if necessary, for the justice they long for which, rightly, they see as theirs.

No 'war on terror' can defeat such an army. No arrogant posturing can drive them away from the bastions of the Western world.

No nation, however strong, can by itself defeat terrorism. It is born of the injustice which disfigures this world.

Only when men learn to share will we see the end of terrorism. Only through sharing can the goal of justice and freedom be realized. Our appeal to you, citizens of the great and blessed United States of America, is to think carefully, and from the heart, as is your wont, when you deliver your vote. Cast your vote for peace, justice and the rule of Law.

October 2004

America's choice

When American citizens go to the polls in November, they will have the opportunity to change the course of history. On their decision largely rests the style and structure of the immediate future. If they choose wisely, they will elect a President committed to fostering the well-being of all who long for peace and justice in our troubled world; who realize that peace and justice are the outcome of trust, and who are prepared to share the vast resources of their country to create that trust.

The alternative is too terrible to contemplate: a mounting programme of war and terror and counter-terror; a tightening grip on the traditional freedoms of the American people; a breakdown of relations with other countries; and a 'pariah' reputation among the nations for the proud United States. Who would knowingly make such a choice?

As the day of destiny approaches, the minds of many turn to the beleaguered people of America whom, now, so many despise and hate. They pray for the deliverance of its people from the cruel and crude exponents of illegal, usurped power. They call for every peace-loving American to raise their voice against the war-mongering of the present administration, and to cast their vote in like fashion.

Of course, America is not alone at fault for the inequalities of the world, the basic canker in our midst, the source of all our troubles. It shares the blame with all the developed countries who ride roughshod and cavalier over the poor and struggling, and must awaken to this main source of tension — and terror.

Therein lies the fault of the Western world: these 'successful' countries owe their wealth and dominance largely to history, and their ability to manipulate the world's economy to their own advantage through aggressive 'market forces'. The world's poor and destitute now demand their share. If this simple right of justice is not addressed and remedied, the world will know no peace. Terrorism will fester and grow into war, which will threaten the future of the people of Earth.

We, your Elder Brothers, cannot stand aside and watch while the very future of the world is under threat. America is a great nation with much of good to give the world. It must now awaken to its soul's longing to serve, to live in peace and justice, and, together, in harmony and co-operation, to work with all nations to remake this world.

This election can be a great turning point in the affairs of men. Cast your vote, We beg you, for justice, sharing and peace.

November 2004

America adrift

It is only a matter of time before the people of the United States realize that they have made a grievous mistake. They have reinstated, albeit with the aid of many stolen votes, a man and administration dedicated to the creation of division and hatred, both nationally and internationally.

They will ruefully watch an attack on their proudly held freedoms; they will see a steep decline in their standard of living as the government, of necessity, strives to tackle their enormous debts; they will witness a loss of confidence in their currency and a sharp reversal of trade with their traditional trading partners. The calamitous invasion of Iraq will continue to fester, both in Iraq and elsewhere in the world. Reacting to the fear and hatred which this administration has engendered almost universally, the tendency will be for the people to look inwards, and to turn their backs even more squarely on the world.

A major problem in dealing with this administration is the powerful illusion under which it works: that it is God-inspired and so in divine Grace, helping to restore the Christian world and message to its former power and glory. Thus has the USA taken a huge step backwards, isolating itself from the true concerns of much of the world: environmental pollution and the demands of a planet suffering under the strain of impending disaster.

The United States will find that the world will not stand still. With or without American co-operation the nations will proceed as best they can to deal with the many ecological and social problems which beset us, and which so urgently must be addressed. America will find itself left behind and ignored, and only then will it be prepared to 'lead' the way.

This administration is, even now, relishing its victory, and weighing the pros and cons of subsequent action.

Thwarted and taken unawares by events in Iraq, it must pause awhile before considering further violence. But the bravado and rhetoric will doubtless continue, hoping to bully and conquer by threats alone. Meanwhile, great changes in many countries are under way, leading to a profound shift in the balance of power in the world. China and India, South America and Russia, are finding their feet and economic potential. Africa is beginning to receive, at last, the concern and goodwill of powerful governments and agencies, and can look forward to better times.

Thus the world is turning away from the dominance of American power and wealth, and charting another path to fulfil its destiny.

If the United States insists on its right of unilateral action, it will find itself neglected and ignored in international plans and projects, its economy will further decay, and its people will lose confidence and trust in government action. Without friends, and with ebbing strength, it will be forced to change, and to renew dialogue with its former friends.

The emergence of Maitreya will speed the process of this transformation and assure its welcome completion.

December 2004

Out of darkness

From time to time, the natural forces of the planet demonstrate their irresistible power in a way destructive and unwelcomed by men.

Thus it was in the recent catastrophe in the Indian Ocean. The sad and sudden loss of thousands of lives, and the unprecedented damage to homes and other buildings, have shocked the world and evoked a remarkable response: for the first time, the nations, East and West, North and South, have come together in spontaneous aid. Governments are prodded by their people to give, and to cancel outstanding debts for the poorest countries. The wave of sympathy for the bereft has manifested also as a concern for the needy millions of all the developing world and is a sure sign that the peoples are ready for Maitreya.

No clearer indication could be given that this is so. No one could doubt the sincerity of this concern; the tragedy of the tsunami has opened the hearts and inspired the voices of millions for the creation of justice and world transformation.

At last, these voices are being heard. At last, the beneficent energies of Maitreya are finding response in the hearts of many still unaware of His presence. At long last, the governments of the wealthy are responding to their people's call for justice and peace. They sense that their future, too, depends on listening to the voice of the people, rising with an ever clearer and powerful note.

Let the governments understand: the voice of the people is the voice of wisdom. It is a call for realism and truth, for the only action which will lead to a sane and better world. Those governments which fail to listen to that voice will founder, and lose authority and the trust of their people.

Maitreya, meanwhile, awaits the moment to emerge, judging finely the pros and cons. He welcomes the signs of men's readiness, and knows that the moment is not far off. He welcomes the opportunity to work openly for humanity and the Plan. In this way, His power and effectiveness are immeasurably increased.

Also, in this way, He can work directly with men, showing His concern for their welfare and comfort, His understanding of their needs and difficulties, His awareness of their problems and of how they can be solved. He wishes to be seen as a brother and friend, a wise father Whose counsel is beneficent and true, a help-mate and partner on the journey into the shining future which awaits all men.

Be patient, therefore, a little longer, and know that despite the problems and difficulties, the heartache of loss, the Plan for the transformation of the world and the salvation of men is on course for victory, and that all will be well.

January/February 2005

Maitreya's task

It is becoming ever clearer that the momentum of change is growing steadily throughout the world. Event follows so quickly on event that few can discern the logic of the sequence by which the new supplants the old. We, your Elder Brothers, recognize the inevitability of this process and watch it with satisfaction, knowing, as We do, that all is moving towards the more perfect expression of the Plan.

For men, however, this is a time of testing and trouble as they seek to understand and cope with the effects of their actions. The logic of happenings escapes them and makes them doubt the divinity in which they place their trust. Thus, for men, has it always been, as they struggle blindly to enforce their will or to escape the consequence of their endeavours.

As we move from age to age, such periods of tension and indecision are repeated again and again. Each new age brings into the world new and unfamiliar forces which gradually impose themselves on men and invoke response. Thus it is today, as men search dimly for the new direction which the new age energies demand of them. Some there are who sense the way and seek to educate their brothers in the required action. Many, though, are afraid of change and see only an impending chaos and breakdown if the 'radicals' have their way.

Into this divided world has come the Christ. His is the task to reconcile these disparate groups and to bring order out of the present confusion and tumult. That His is not an easy task should be apparent to all. That the gulf between the groups is vast and entrenched is equally clear. How, then, must He work to bridge the chasm between the old and fearful and the burgeoning new? How, too, can He counter the deep materialism which is the hallmark of the

35

present time? How deal with the intolerance of the religious groups and help them to experience unity?

Presenting Himself as a man among men, Maitreya will make no claims, demand no allegiance. Simple and direct will be His approach, moderate and calm His manner. His clarity of mind will arrest attention. His wisdom will overcome men's fears. His sincerity of utterance will melt men's hearts and remove the burden of hate and greed. Thus will men experience a new appearance of divinity, one which includes them in its manifestation, and sees no distance or separation.

As the Embodiment and Agent of cosmic power and love, Maitreya will open the hearts of all who can respond, and, turning men from the fear and division of the past, ready them for the glory of the future.

March 2005

The end of corruption

More and more, the nations are beginning to recognize, to take seriously and to deal with, an age-old problem, namely corruption. In some parts of the world corruption has been a way of life for centuries. This has benefited the few, of course, at the expense of the many. For untold ages, corrupt leaders and powerful politicians have waxed rich on the taxes imposed on their subjects and citizens. In modern times, the large corporations of the West have been found guilty of 'cooking the books' on a massive scale, while in the East it is taken for granted that every transaction needs the 'greasing' of someone's palm.

Corruption is endemic, and runs through some societies from the president or prime minister to the police and sport. Electoral corruption is rampant, as recent elections have demonstrated, even in countries supposedly dedicated to freedom and democracy. Such corrupt governments fail and betray their peoples and so surrender their right to govern.

In the midst of such corruption is it possible to engender trust without which the future for men would be bleak indeed? Without trust, a fairer sharing of resources would be a forlorn hope. Without trust, the global decisions required to sustain our planetary home would never be taken. Without blessed and beneficent trust, men would forfeit their right of Stewardship of Planet Earth, and would seal themselves off for aeons from further evolution.

Thus would it be, and thus should men tackle seriously, and without delay, the corrosive impact of corruption on every strata of society, and every nook and cranny of our planetary life.

To help men to do this, you may be sure that Maitreya will be at pains to demonstrate to men the eroding effect of corruption in all its many manifestations. He will show that if men would become the Gods they essentially are, they must abandon the old ways of deceit and subterfuge. To tackle the serious environmental problems, He will explain, men must work together, in trust. Without trust, Maitreya will emphasize, little can be done. So steeped in corruption themselves are the leaders of the nations, that they trust no one.

Maitreya will show that men have but one choice to create the necessary trust: to share the produce of this bounteous Earth more evenly across the world, and so end for ever the starvation and poverty of millions, dying in the midst of plenty.

Will the leaders listen to the words of Maitreya? For the most part, possibly, no, not at first. But soon the people everywhere will hear, and see the wisdom of Maitreya's advice. They will say amen to His wise words and support His Cause. World public opinion will find its voice and its Mentor, and against its power the obstructive voices of the greedy dictators and corrupt politicians will fade. So will it be, and so will begin the cleansing and transformation of this world.

April 2005

The achievement of men

Every century, and every twenty-five years of the century, We, the Masters of Wisdom, gather together to assess the success or otherwise of the many projects and plans which We have previously set in motion. In this way We know how well certain plans are faring and, if not, can make the necessary adjustments and changes before harm is done.

This may seem to some a slow and ponderous rhythm but Our long experience tells Us that evolution proceeds slowly and humanity takes long to build in, and stabilize, the necessary advances. Advance, however, is sure if the Plan is carefully followed and We have much faith in Our methods.

As We look back on the twentieth century We see an astonishing picture. Truly it was one of titanic struggle and achievement, a veritable battleground for warring forces so opposed and committed. It saw humanity at last, battleweary but triumphant, come of age. From Our perspective, last century saw humanity reach adulthood, ready to take decisions and to think its own way forward. The trials and tribulations were many and daunting, calling out from men the best that was in them, preparing them for the decisions which lie immediately ahead.

The two world wars of the past century saw humanity divide itself in two: those who, for all their faults, stood on the side of Light, for freedom and justice for all and the democratic ideal; and those who worshipped power for its own sake, who stood on the dark side of life and sought to enslave the minds and hearts of those weaker than themselves. The triumph of the Forces of Light ensures that men know better the reality in which they live, and the nature of the materialism against which they fought so bitterly and at such cost. Thus was forged a sense of the grandeur of human life and also of its sacredness and worth.

It is this achievement which has made possible the re-entry into the world of the Christ and His group of Masters. The events of the twentieth century have been momentous. They constitute the major trials of the World Disciple and shown him ready, when led by Us, to battle against and conquer tyranny, to right the wrongs of the past and to grasp the fact of Brotherhood in all its beauty.

Some, surveying the world and the actions of small but ambitious men, doubt that this is possible. They see only the outer, transient events and not the changes wrought on men under the laws of evolution. Our hopes for men are high. This is said not lightly for We know that much needs still to be done to ensure the future for men and planet. Our view of men is based on long association with the trials and tests of life which have brought men to readiness to inherit their destiny.

May 2005

Man's inheritance

When the dust has settled on the present world situation a very interesting picture will present itself to the perceptive viewer. It will be a picture which, in many respects, runs contrary to the general understanding and apprehensions of many today. It is true that there are many dangerous tensions and divisions which need insight and care to resolve; there are also many problems which defy men's wisdom to overcome, and which need an entirely new approach, so far lacking. Equally, however, there are many signs of progress and new realization on the part of men, many instances of a new and mature wisdom in tackling the difficulties and uncertainties which surround them. The panorama of life is not flat and one dimensional but is a changing arena of stratified events, moving simultaneously and in many directions.

Thus, it is necessary to observe the main, and general, trends to understand the true happenings of the time. When one can do so a different picture emerges of the present world scene and its probable outcome.

Far from fulfilling the fears of so many today the future, We believe, offers men the greatest possibility of progress and growth of consciousness that, as a race, they have ever enjoyed. Nothing like the coming opportunity has ever been presented to men. Never have so many been ready to respond to that felicitous time. Never have We, your Elder Brothers, been so sure of the outcome, and so firm in Our resolve to work with men and to aid them in every way We can.

We approach Our task, not lightly but light of heart and eager of mind, as We enter your lives to teach and to tend.

We invite you to listen to what We have to say and to work with Us on your behalf. In this way, you will make fewer mistakes and avoid blind alleys. Thus will the work of change and reconstruction be unhindered and sure, and thus can all men take their places at Our side and learn the arts of peace and love.

We are entering your lives not solely for men's guidance but also as a step in Our own evolution; nevertheless, Our main effort will be spent in helping men overcome the difficulties and mistakes of the past, and to make best use of the opportunities presented to them as the new era unfolds. We have every confidence that men, in their turn, will show themselves to be apt and responsive pupils; that the light of knowledge and wisdom that We bring will find resonance in their hearts and minds; that when Justice has brought blessed Peace, men will awaken to the ancient truths again and see that all men are One, now and for ever; and, following that banner, will transform, gladly and quickly, the fabric of life on Earth into the shining vision which We know to be man's inheritance.

June 2005

The end of darkness

Nowhere is division and disharmony more prevalent than on Planet Earth. No other planet of our system is so immersed in competition, so ignorant of the benefits of cooperation. Nowhere else is seen the results of such folly: anxiety, illness of all kinds; wealth and poverty side by side, insecurity and war.

Why should this be so? Why should the inhabitants of this most richly fertile world quarrel so over its ownership?

To some extent the answer lies in the very richness of Earth's resources. Earth is the most densely material of worlds and for long ages men have been in thrall to its material wealth, and have fought and competed for its control. This has brought the human kingdom (and with it the animal) to the verge of destruction. With the nuclear bomb man has brought his very existence into jeopardy.

It is this fact above all which has prompted Maitreya's decision to return with His group to the everyday world, at least a thousand years ahead of the planned date. His aim is to coax men back from the brink, to show them how dangerous and destructive is their lust for power, their greed and competition.

He will outline for them a simpler way, the way of cooperation, justice and trust.

Many there are today who, in their hearts, renounce the iniquities of the present materialism which pervades the planet. They long for justice and peace and march and demonstrate for their fulfilment. More and more, the peoples of the world are beginning to recognize that together they have the power to change the actions of powerful men. Thus does Maitreya trust the people and gives voice to their demands. Thus does He join their marches and adds His voice to theirs.

Amid the general avarice there is, too, an awakening of conscience among politicians and others in several countries. The debts of the poorest nations are being cancelled and a new approach to the grinding poverty of so many is taking place. The fruits of twenty years of labour are beginning to ripen. Maitreya's beneficent energies are working their magic and a new spirit is gaining strength.

Thus the attitudes and habits of countless ages are beginning to crumble before the tide of new and unstoppable energies wielded by Maitreya and His group. Men need have no fear; the meek, indeed, the poor, the powerless, the toilers everywhere, shall inherit the Earth. Men will learn the beauty of co-operation and service and one by one the bastions of power will fall. The empires of power and wealth will disappear as the new urge for sharing and oneness grips the minds of men. Thus will it be and thus will man regain his sanity and start the climb again.

July/August 2005

The guidance of Maitreya

However much they may try, politicians and other leaders find it more and more difficult to control events and to keep their 'ship of state' on an even keel. They find that, despite their expertise, it careers helplessly on its own as if under the guidance of some unseen hand. That unseen hand, of course, is the logic of change. They fail to understand that the rules and methods by which they work belong to the past and have little relevance to the problems and needs of today. They meet and discuss these problems, but invariably retreat from actions that alone would solve them. Meanwhile, in varying degrees, the people suffer, and wait for reason and insight to alleviate their distress. They know in their hearts that deliverance is possible and should be theirs, but lack, as yet, the structures and power to make it so.

Not for ever will the people wait. Already, the signs of dissent and impatience are appearing across the world, urging the leaders to engage with their needs and afflictions. The leaders, men without vision, look to promises and palliatives to halt the mounting demands for fairness and justice. They do so in vain. The peoples of the world have caught the vision of freedom, of justice, and peace, and will not let it go. They, rather than their leaders, will outline the future and shape it to their needs. Thus will it be. This new force in the world — the voice of the people — is rapidly gaining strength and cohesion and will play a major role in world affairs from now.

Maitreya awaits His opportunity to augment the power and influence of the people's voice and to steer its course. Many are the strands which form it and disparate their aim. Wise must be the guidance, therefore, lest it lose its way and dissipate its strength.

Single and simple, therefore, must be the demands of the people. Many and varied are their problems but universal are their needs: peace through justice and freedom are the needs of all men. Sharing, Maitreya will advise, is the key to the creation of trust without which naught is possible. Share and make blessed trust, He will tell the world, and know the blessings of justice and peace. No other way, He will solemnly remind the nations, will bring them the peace for which in their hearts they yearn. Thus will it be, and thus will the people call for sharing and therefore peace. A new and potent world opinion will demonstrate its power and render obsolete the manoeuvres and stratagems of the men of power today. Then will Maitreya declare Himself to all the peoples, and dedicate Himself to their service throughout this coming time.

September 2005

The Brotherhood of Man

Sooner or later, the reality of their interdependence will dawn upon the nations and their leaders. This realization will bring about an entirely new attitude to the problems with which, today, they wrestle, and will lead to easier, and wiser, solutions of these difficulties. A gradual change in outlook will replace the present fierce competition and confrontation with mutual understanding and co-operation. That not all nations will proceed in this direction at the same pace, must be said, but the effectiveness and obvious sanity of the method will encourage even the least sanguine, eventually, to see the benefits for all. Each step forward will cement this process and hasten the movement towards co-operation. In this way, a healthier relationship will evolve between the nations, leading in time to a true sense of brotherhood.

Many smaller nations recognize, already, the reality of interdependence but lacking power their voices go unheard. Large and powerful nations scorn such notions, their pride in self-sufficiency blinding them to the truth of their relationship with the world.

Man evolves but slowly and needs time and experiment to make significant advance, but precisely in this way do these achievements become stable and permanent.

The United Nations is, of course, the forum in which the voice of the smaller nations can be raised and heard. This is only possible when the Security Council, with its arbitrary veto, is abolished. It has outlasted its usefulness and must soon give way to a United Nations Assembly free of the abuses of power and veto.

Then will we see the nations acting without restraints imposed by Great Power veto and financial inducement. Those who call loudest for democracy in foreign lands are strangely blind to its absence in the halls of the United Nations.

Men must come to realize that the people of all the nations are one and equal, dependent each upon the other. No one nation owns, nor can rule, the world. No one nation can stand alone against the rest. The days of empire and dominion are past. Man is on the threshold of a new understanding of his role on planet Earth. This involves a change in his relationship to his fellow travellers on the path to wisdom and true stewardship of the planet's bounty.

We, your Elder Brothers, will help men to make this change. Maitreya will set before men the alternative to action and the transformation of the world. He will show that without a change of direction the future would be difficult and bleak indeed. He will also inspire men to realize their interdependence, the reality of their Brotherhood.

October 2005

The key to the future

It is with sadness that We watch the continuing efforts of men to solve their problems with the methods of the past. These problems are many and relate to the future as much as to the present. In the main, they are relics of the past and represent a heavy burden for the burgeoning societies of today. Lost in their fierce battle for markets, governments everywhere try all the standard ways to achieve security and strength, development and innovation, and stability in the midst of change. It is an impossible task.

There is but one answer to all their troubles, one solution to all their problems, yet none, so far, has ventured to whisper the word which, at a stroke, would free them and the world. Which, at one stroke, would launch this world into the new era of Righteousness and Truth. Let the word resound, let the word demonstrate the new civilization, the new society. Let the word be heard everywhere; let man respond.

The word is the sound of righteousness, it is the sound of truth. The word brings all men together, and builds the Brotherhood of men. The word sits lightly on the heart, bringing happiness to all. The word is wise and generous, filled with love. The word is sharing, the key to the future.

Sharing is the answer to all men's problems. Sharing is another word for divinity. Sharing initiates the highest that is possible for man for it opens the door to trust. Sharing will take men to the feet of God.

When men learn to share they will know the meaning of life. When men share they will feel exalted and love what they do. Sharing will make men whole. Sharing will make man One.

There is no end to the concept of sharing. It will prove the salvation of men.

When men see Maitreya they will hear these words of Truth. They will listen to His pronouncements with wide-open hearts, and, responding, will call for the end of tyranny and injustice. They will gather around Him and He will be their spokesman. Soon, men will see His face. Soon, He will present His ideas to the world and usher out the old age.

He is near men now. He cannot be denied. His love now saturates the planes and brings change to the fore.

Consider this: without Maitreya's help man is doomed. We earnestly await the response from men.

November 2005

The beginning of the new time

Patiently, We, your Elder Brothers, await the response of men, knowing, as We do so, that the vast majority of people, when they know and understand the true situation now present on Earth, will agree that only radical change will forestall calamity.

One problem has been that the average person knows little of the enormous vested interests which control the affairs of men, and which, for the most part, work against the needs and rights of countless millions. At the moment, 80 per cent of the world's wealth is owned by a small number of families and institutions. Much of that wealth is 'static', invested in estates, ships, gold, jewels and works of art, benefiting thereby but few. Such imbalance confounds the efforts of governments everywhere to establish societies based on relative social justice.

So old and so entrenched is this imbalance that only a Herculean effort or world economic disaster will shake its hold. Faced with this situation, governments are at a loss to manage their nation's affairs and, simultaneously, compete with others for markets. The result, inevitably, is recurring chaos, instability, and a chronic lack of money for essential services and foreign aid. The world's poor continue to suffer, therefore, and pray silently for change. Some, less silent, join the growing number of the world's terrorist groups.

How then to break this vicious circle of inherited wealth, stagnation and revolutionary hatred and violence?

Maitreya, on His emergence, will address this problem and show its mechanism and negative effect on all aspects of life, national and international. He will show that only a just and fair distribution of the world's wealth will realize the peace that all desire. That sharing alone will create the trust that makes such a distribution possible. That men have no alternative: all other ways have been tried and have failed — and the sands are running out.

Thus will the Great One speak. Thus will He raise the consciousness of men and help them to understand the reasons for their plight. He will show that such imbalance is insupportable in a world so interdependent and facing so many perilous problems. That only a rational transformation of our now defunct structures will allow men to advance into the future and to build a civilization worthy of the name.

When men hear His words they will divide into three groups: one will, with full heart, respond to His thoughts and answer His appeal for their engagement. One will form a blockade of opposition and affront. A third, smaller, number will sit, anxiously, aside.

Gradually, it will become obvious that change must be tried, at least, and some experiments will be undertaken. This will convince many of the feasibility of sharing and lead to the Day of Declaration, the signal that the New Time has begun.

December 2005

The wonder at the door

There will soon come a time when men will know, beyond all dispute, that the Christ is once more among us. People of all faiths await Him as the Holy One, the Knower of God. Men will come to know Him as a Brother and Teacher Who will vouchsafe for them their divinity. At present, He awaits patiently the moment of His emergence to work for, and before, the world. Yet even as He waits He works ceaselessly for all men. Not for one second does He remove His gaze or withhold His love. Moment to moment that love embraces all who can absorb it and enters their hearts by stealth. So does He uphold the world of men, protecting and wisely guiding. Be prepared to see a brother but one Who has entered a new state of Brotherhood, come to aid and to teach, and by His love to redeem.

The time is short before His open appearance. Take heart from this and quicken your service on His behalf. Make known that He is among you and stir the hearts of those who know not yet these glad tidings. Fulfil your purpose and redeem the promise which you, long ago, have made.

The world waits, alert, expectant, knowing not the reason for its hope. The world, too, groans in misery and fear, longing for succour and the end of anguish. Maitreya will show that the time has come to address the age-long problems that keep men apart, that create rich and poor, that engender war and the ailing of our planet. He will show, too, that time is shortening daily to tend our planet back to health.

Maitreya will teach men the reason for their presence on Earth and the method of fulfilling that purpose. He will show that within each one exists a Being of Light and inspire them to become that Being. He will remind them that nothing stands between themselves and God but ignorance and fear. He will release men from their guilt and turn them to joy. He will show men that guiltless and fearless they will know love.

Understand well that this is a time like none other, never to be repeated. It is a time heroic, valorous and sacred. Use this time to strengthen your links with each other and Maitreya. Work for Him as never before. Be not afraid, for the time is soon when you will see Him and know that you have not worked in vain.

Thus it is, friends and workers in the Light. Cast far that light and awaken your brothers and sisters who know not yet the wonder which is afoot in this, our world.

January/February 2006

The ending of war

When the time comes to count the cost, men will be amazed at, and ashamed of, the waste of war. More than any other activity of men, war eats greedily into resources and lives. Nothing is spared in the effort to overcome the 'enemy'; everything is sacrificed to the attainment of victory. Thus has man waged relentless strife against his neighbour, and not always in self-defence. As often as not, war has been used for the expansion of territory, the accumulation of plunder or, most abhorrently, the capture of slaves. The 'spoils of war' is a phrase used lightly to describe the underlying purpose of most wars.

Today, we have reached a time when men must take seriously the task of ending war. Men must understand that there is no problem or situation which needs war to solve or cure. This being so the nations must together act and end for ever that destructive aptitude of men.

Should they fail to do so, they threaten the very existence of the race. Peace is no longer an option for men: they have now in their hands the deadliest weapon of all time which, if used in major war, would desecrate the planet and leave it lifeless for aeons of time. Why, then, court such disaster, such an end?

Maitreya, you may be sure, will speak thus on His emergence. He will show men that small wars can lead to terrible consequences, and set men on the slippery slope of self-destruction. He will counsel gravely and turn men from the unthinkable. Be vigilant but not afraid; trust Maitreya to wisely guide the actions of men. Play your part in the task of educating your brothers and sisters and so make lighter His burden.

Tell all who will listen that the Expected One is here, ready to begin, openly, His Mission. That He relies on the men and women of goodwill to work with Him for peace and justice, freedom and love. Tell them this. Tell them that Maitreya has the simple answer for the world's woes. That sharing will engender the trust that will open the door, and the hearts of men, to blessed peace.

Then will you see the flowering of the human spirit in brotherhood and co-operation. Then will the problems and blockages melt away, overcome in overflowing goodwill.

Thus will it be, and thus shall we witness the end of the abomination of war. Such is Maitreya's purpose and firm is His will for its accomplishment.

March 2006

Signs in abundance

Whenever, as now, man is in a quandary, unsure whether to go forward or back, to the left or the right, there emerges an interesting phenomenon: signs are looked for, even by those who do not believe in signs; unexplainable happenings are taken seriously and given meaning; men search for the key that will open the door through which they must go to the future, unsure, as yet, of what that future may hold for them.

The signs that would guide them are there in abundance but men soon forget the wonders which have been lavished on them for many years. Thus, in the main, men miss the very indications for which they search and for which they beg.

The time is soon coming when men will remember the signs and accept them as true portents of the days to come. They will understand them as a planned manifestation synchronized with the emergence of Maitreya and His group of Masters at this unique time in the history of the world. Many and varied have been these signals to men that something momentous and wonderful is afoot on Earth. For those with eyes to see, they have stood as a reminder to man that there are many areas of life that remain unknown and mysterious, that there are laws of which men know but little, and, above all, that man is not alone.

Since there are signs, there are creators of the signs. All religious groups await and expect their chosen divine revelation and read the signs as confirmation of their faith. Such confirmation sustains them in perilous times and gives them hope for a better future. In this way a climate of expectancy and hope is created among many millions and prepares them for the events which now are imminent. Few can deny the signs although their meaning may be obscure.

They quicken the intuition and the imagination of men and open their hearts to the revelations which are to come.

From statues which weep and move to light patterns which adorn the fronts of buildings across the world; from shining crosses of light to milk-drinking Hindu gods, the signs are endless. Few can have been untouched by these wonders.

Doubters and sceptics, of course, are ever to be found. But not for long. Very soon, the climate of expectancy will grow and register firmly in the minds and hearts of men everywhere, and into that expectant atmosphere Maitreya will enter and begin His open mission. Thus will it be.

April 2006

Unity in diversity

Throughout the centuries, men have adopted many different forms of government, ranging from the most despotic to the most egalitarian. Today, most countries have opted for a democratic form, that is, one elected by popular vote for one or other political party. It is assumed that the voting system used is fair, honest, free from malpractice and fraud.

Unfortunately, as recent history shows, this is often not the case, even in those countries which lay great stress on the probity of their election process. Deception and duplicity abound, men and factions are brought to power by chicanery and guile.

More authoritarian are those one-party states where decisions are made by a committee of 'strong men' backed by the army and police. The people have little say in the laws which rule them and often, as yet, do not feel the need to claim such rights.

Some countries are in the grip of cruel despots, hungry for power and the wealth which comes with it. Some are ruled by deluded zealots, sure that they and their followers are in the hands of God and are carrying out His plans. Others are struggling to help their people out of poverty and pain, and to fend off the demands of their wealthy neighbours.

Still others are fighting for their independence or are engulfed in chaos and civil war.

Men must take to heart the lesson from this evidence: many are the ways of organizing the needs of different peoples. Greater tolerance, therefore, is necessary in the approach to this vital matter. The energies of the rays governing the nations are different and require different structures in which to express their qualities. It is not the evolutionary Plan that one form of government, democratic or otherwise, should prevail. The needs of men are more real and more important than ideologies. Tolerance of difference unites, while ideologies divide.

When Maitreya speaks openly, therefore, He will show that unity in diversity is the key to future harmony. That all the nations have a destiny, unique and sacred. He will point the way to achieve this blessed state and encourage men to open their hearts to a wiser understanding of the Plan. Under Maitreya's guidance, men will come to appreciate and value the richness of the achievements of themselves and others. The urge to compete and to dominate will gradually subside and a new chapter will open for men in brotherhood and peace. Thus will it be.

May 2006

Invisible peril

If men were to see the state of the world as We, the Masters, see, they would be amazed, dumfounded and afraid, all at the same time. So far from the reality is man's view of conditions on Earth, and so lacking in judgement is he about future possibilities, that, without help, man would watch his planetary home languish and die.

As it is, planet Earth is in a sad and perilous condition while each day brings it nearer to the critical. Many voices have sounded warnings on global warming, and many views have been expressed, but even the most dire prophecy falls short of the calamity facing the world today. Few there are who see the immediacy of the threat and the urgency of the steps needed to counter it.

Great as is the peril posed by global warming, this, unfortunately, is not the greatest, or most hazardous, faced by man today. Did he but know it, man is engaged in a slow but steadily increasing intoxification of the race and of the lower kingdoms. Toxicity, pollutions, of all kinds, and in all fields, is now the greatest danger to men, animals and the Earth itself. All are poisoned and sick in their own way.

Unknown to men but evident to Us, the greatest harm sustained by men and planet in this sorry tale is caused by nuclear radiation. Men have gone far astray in the development of this most dangerous energetic source. Led astray by greed, and the false hope of vast profits, they have concentrated their experiments in 'taming' the most dangerous source of energy ever discovered by man, neglecting, meanwhile, a perfectly safe alternative use of the energy of the atom. Atomic fusion, cold and harmless, could be theirs from a simple isotope of water, everywhere available in the oceans, seas and rivers, and in every shower of rain.

Man must cease his 'toying with death'. Atomic fission is the result of the atomic bombs which destroyed Hiroshima and Nagasaki; which erupted in Chernobyl and causes, subtly, death and sickness today. It is "that which stands where it ought not" and which must be renounced by man if he would prosper further.

Earth scientists are confident that they have, indeed, tamed the monster, and can keep it under control. They do not realize that their instruments are crude indeed, that they measure only the lower aspects of nuclear radiation, that stretching above these dense-physical levels are levels finer and more dangerous to the health and well-being of all. But for the tireless efforts of our Extra-planetary Brothers in assuaging this invisible peril in so far as the karmic law allows, our plight would be perilous indeed. Wake up, mankind!

June 2006

The path of Love and Peace

Fortunately for man, he is never left without help when it is needed. However difficult the circumstances, however great and grave the dangers which he faces, of one thing he can be sure: he will never be abandoned by his Elder Brothers. Time after time in men's long history, when all seemed lost and the future of man perilously unsure, Our succour has been forthcoming and the forward path of men restored once more. So it is today at this tumultuous time when men stand in a maelstrom of warring forces, unsure of the next step and all but overwhelmed by the enormity of the task ahead.

Emerging from Our ancient retreats, We redirect Our thoughts and steps to aid Our struggling brothers. To show, by example, that all is not lost, that another, and better, way exists for men to organize their lives; that unity and happiness come from justice and freedom; that sharing is the natural action of unity and the simple answer to all man's woes.

Men must desire the gift of Wisdom We have to give. The Great Law does not allow its imposition. Thus do men require to look clearly at the dangers which beset them, and so make their decision and choice.

That men need guidance is beyond dispute (though many would deny that this is so or possible to find) and this guidance will Maitreya, Himself, offer to men for their consideration and wise counsel.

Responding, men must see themselves as One. The old barriers to freedom and justice must be discarded; all must share in the Earth's bounty; all must learn the language of trust. Planet Earth, our home, must be nursed back to health, its air, soil and waters purified, made safe again for man.

These are the urgent requirements for the stabilization of the Planet and the health of its inhabitants. Once adopted, there will be no return to the disorder of the past. Man will part company with poverty and war, exploitation and cruelty, corruption and injustice. Men will emulate their Elder Brothers and walk the path of Love and Peace.

See this time as the time of Decision. All rests on man's response to Maitreya's counsel. We, your Elder Brothers, are neither anxious nor complacent. We know the enormous task that faces both Maitreya and men. We also know how to read the Signs of Life and are not afraid. Be you who read this not afraid but spread abroad the fact that the Restoration of Earth is at hand, that the iniquities of the past are fading and with them the old ways of governance. A new Guidance is here to show the way for men, an ancient but ever new Guidance to take men to the Mountain Top.

July/August 2006

Help is needed – and offered

It will soon become clear that without help men have but little time to rectify the problems, ecological, political and economic which cause chaos, danger and heartache to the majority of Earth's people. It is a situation unique in Earth's history. Much depends on men realizing that they have, as custodians, the responsibility to tend carefully the well-being of the planet and all its kingdoms, and to pass on a vibrant, healthy planetary home to future generations. So unhealthy has the planet become from man's predatory action and cavalier neglect, that, were it human, grave doubts of its recovery would be in order. The home of man and the lower kingdoms must be nursed back to health to fulfil its role in the evolving Plan.

Chaos reigns, likewise, in the political sphere. The nations are led by groups dedicated to the past, unable to see that their methods apply no longer to the needs of today and tomorrow. Blindfolded and arrogant, they strut the stage of life like out-of-date actors, unsure of their direction or their lines. The door marked EXIT looms large for these destructive usurpers of power.

The economic and social spheres are the saddest of all. While the world's wealth flows into fewer and fewer hands, countless millions beg for the minimum to survive. Millions are too weak to beg, and die, forlorn, before they have tasted life. What can men do to rectify these sad and dangerous conditions? To whom can they turn for help in their agony?

There is but one source of help for men in their extreme need. That help is theirs for the asking. We, your Elder Brothers, seek only your welfare and happiness, and are ready to aid you and to point the way to a better future for all.

We see all men as One, brothers and sisters of one great family. Men need, likewise, to banish from their hearts the sense of separation, and to rediscover the reality of brotherhood which lies at the heart of the human condition. Men, all men, are potential Gods and needs must create the conditions in which they all can flourish. We will help you to do this, gladly, when you take the first small step in that direction. That first step is not difficult nor fraught with risk. You have nothing to lose and your divinity to gain: that first step is called Sharing.

September 2006

Maitreya's priorities

While the world waits, expectantly, for Maitreya, and deliverance, there still remains much to do to secure the planet and mankind. Nevertheless, men have little time to wait for Maitreya to begin His open service. Short, indeed, therefore, is the time left to prepare His way, to tell men that help and hope are at hand, that the Teacher is here, eager to speak directly to the peoples of all the nations.

Speed, then, your efforts. Make haste to inform all who will listen that the destined hour has arrived, that soon mankind will rejoice in the presence of the Teacher. Tell them this and uphold their hope and courage. Many will listen now who before did not; anxiety and fear have taken their toll of men. The signs, too, have done their work and awakened millions to expected happenings and revelations. Never before in man's history have so many sensed the coming changes nor understood their necessity.

Hence, into an expectant and prepared world will Maitreya emerge, sure in the knowledge that His presence is longed for and eagerly anticipated.

Maitreya will outline for men the priorities which alone will secure and safeguard planet Earth and all its peoples. The necessity of peace is paramount for without peace all else is lost. Peace, He will affirm, can only be ensured through the creation of Justice. The lack of Justice is the begetter of both war and terrorism. Justice, Maitreya will maintain, can be achieved only through Sharing. Sharing, therefore, is the key to world peace and security.

Maitreya will turn the minds of men more urgently to the ills of planet Earth, itself. Without a healthy and robust planet the future of succeeding generations is in peril. Maitreya will stress the urgency of action now to restore equilibrium to our suffering planetary home, and call all hands, old and young, to this primary task.

The fate of those who now starve in a world of plenty will exercise Maitreya's chief concern: "Nothing so moves Me to grief as this shame," He says, and seeks to galvanize the creation of a vast programme of aid for the world's poor on a scale hitherto unknown.

These are the immediate priorities, to make fast and secure the future for men. Man's free will is sacrosanct and may not be infringed; the speed of implementation of these primary requirements is subject, therefore, to the will of men.

Men now face the choice: to see the world as One and share, and know security and blessed Peace and happiness, or to witness the end of life on Earth.

Maitreya is emerging now to ensure that man's choice is wisely made. Have no fear, Maitreya already knows man's answer, and is glad.

October 2006

The first steps

When Maitreya appears before the world people will realize that they have known Him from before, and that His teaching is not strange or beyond their level of thought. Simple, indeed, will He be that all may understand.

Precisely His simplicity will astound. Nevertheless it will be found also that most people will experience what they hear in a new way, as a dawning truth, new and touching them at a deeper level. Simple the ideas may be, but they will resonate in people's hearts and feel fresh and vibrant. Thus will it be. Thus will Maitreya touch the hearts of men, appealing to them to aid themselves by aiding their brothers and sisters across the world. When men hear Him they will ponder deeply on what He says, and feel strangely moved by the oft-heard words. Their hearts will respond as hitherto they have not, and a new understanding and urgency will potentize their response.

Thus will Maitreya galvanize the peoples of the world to action and change. Those who have stood back will come forward and join the clamour for justice and sharing, freedom and peace.

Many, of course, will ignore Maitreya. Many will find His ideas abhorrent and dangerous or utopian and impossible of accomplishment. Some, more sinister and afraid, will see in Him the antichrist, the embodiment of all their fears. Some would have Him crucified forthwith had they the power. Many will sit quietly on the fence, unable to take a stand, for or against.

Those who can respond will grow in number and raise their voices for sharing and justice. They will gather round and support Him, and see Him as their leader and mentor, teacher and guide.

Thus will form a powerful mass of world public opinion, calling for change. More and more, governments will find it difficult to resist these demands of the people and will be forced to implement some degree of change.

The people will grow in power and their voices, potentized by Maitreya, will grow in strength and clarity of demand. They will call for their Spokesman to speak to the world and the stage will be set for the Day of Declaration, the first day of the New Dawn.

The Day of Declaration, on which, for the first time, Maitreya will acknowledge His true stature and name, will stand out, through history, as the turning point in the evolution of mankind. It will be inscribed in the annals as the Day of Days, the Beginning of the New, the Sanctification of Mankind, the Portal to the glorious future which awaits humanity. That day is not far off.

November 2006

The futility of war

When men engage in war, they endanger not only their own and others' lives, but also the well-being of the planet on which they depend for life itself. The Earth is plundered recklessly for the metals of all kinds used in the ordnance of death. No thought is given to the needs of future generations who also have the right to the planet's bounty. Countless millions of tons of twisted, rusting iron adorn the 'theatres of war' where men enact their deadly pageantry. Men cannot see, or even imagine, the devastation caused to their subtle bodies by endless hours of bombardment. The unprecedented levels of noise tear and shred these sensitive veils. The human frame is not constructed for such abuse. Thus do they do themselves irreparable harm. How long, therefore, will it take men to realize the futility of war? War solves no problem; it creates only chaos, and halts the progress of man.

Some, few, men, it must be said, relish the act of war. It is, for them, an act of valour, a test of their will and skill, but mainly, today, men are drawn into war for ideological reasons, for the cause. Hence it is the leaders of the nations who hold the reins of power, who legislate for war or peace. They must be carefully chosen to ensure a peaceful world.

Much thought must now be given to this problem. Recent events in the Middle East have shown how simple it is to transgress the rule of Law and let loose chaos; to rectify the transgression and bring resolution is quite another matter.

Maitreya watches these events with care. He calculates precisely the tensions and their relaxation as they occur and seeks always to establish equilibrium. In this respect, the energies of the Spirit of Peace or Equilibrium, focused through Maitreya, play a vital part. Potent and precise, they are turning the tide of hatred and warring instincts which so trouble the peoples of the nations.

The people themselves are beginning to play their part. Through ballot-box and demonstration they are making their voices heard, their demands for peace known. From this point there is no turning back. The people are sensing their power and are coming to understand that *they* must *make* the peace they all desire, and that only when justice reigns with freedom will blessed peace be assured.

This growing understanding will set the scene for Maitreya's early emergence.

December 2006

Maitreya steps forward

The emergence of Maitreya is all but accomplished. His open, public work will commence really very soon. From then will begin the process of teaching and becoming known, gradually, to the peoples of the world. The time that this will take remains unclear, but it should proceed relatively quickly. At first, of course, there may be much opposition to His views and the nature of His advice. This is only to be expected, so far from the prevailing thinking is His thought. Gradually, however, Maitreya's incisive mind will cut through and expose the flaws in present beliefs about the environment and on matters social, economic and political. The logic and wise understanding of His words will convince many to listen and contemplate further, while His Ray will penetrate the hearts of millions and turn His simple words into revelations of Truth. No one, as yet, knows the loving power of Maitreya, nor can men fathom His inscrutable wisdom.

As millions rally to His cause, demanding peace and justice through sharing and understanding, men will be swept up and galvanized by new hope and a longing for brotherhood and right relationship. They will demand change on a scale hitherto unknown. The governments and men of power will be forced to respond to the demands, and bit by bit, the edifice against change will crumble before the onslaught of a now empowered voice of public opinion. Thus, by logic, revelation and the trust engendered by His love, will Maitreya harness the goodwill which exists, even if unknown, in every heart.

Maitreya will speak to millions of men through television and radio. All will have the opportunity to share in His blessing which will accompany every appearance. Thus the people worldwide will become familiar with His message and the uplifting of their hearts. Much speculation will surround His identity and many will be the theories presented, but all in their different ways will see Him as the harbinger of the new, a conveyor of wholesome truths and as a way-shower of a lifestyle close to their hearts.

Of course, there will be those who feel threatened by His ideas, and who will attempt to stop His progress but, more and more, the beauty and good sense of His words will inspire the people of all the nations to see Him as their spokesman and leader. Thus will it be. The people will call for Him to speak on their behalf to the world at large, and the Day of Declaration will be announced.

This day, like none other before or after, will give Maitreya the opportunity to reveal His name, title and purpose, as the World Teacher for the New Age, the leader of the Spiritual Hierarchy and the Expected One of all religious groups. As the friend and teacher of all who need His help will He present Himself; as a simple man Who knows the pain and suffering of men and seeks to ease their lot, Who loves all totally, without condition, and Who has come to show us the steps to joy.

Such a one is about to step before the world and give His advice to all. We may have heard the words before. Now, with His blessing, we shall understand their meaning, and act.

January/February 2007

The gathering of the Forces of Light

Important events are taking place in many parts of the world. People everywhere will be astonished by the reports. These will include sightings, in unprecedented numbers, of spacecraft from our neighbouring planets, Mars and Venus in particular. Nothing like this increased activity, over vast areas of the Earth, will have been seen before. Those who have steadfastly refused to take seriously the reality of this phenomenon will find it difficult to deny. More and more accounts of contact with the occupants of the spacecraft will add their testimony to the fact of their existence. Miraculous happenings of all kinds will continue and multiply in number and variety. The minds of men will be baffled and amazed by these wonders, and this will cause them to ponder deeply.

Into this wonder-filled, wondering world Maitreya will quietly enter and begin His open work. He will be asked to counter their doubts and fears, to explain these happenings and He will vouchsafe their validity. These extraordinary events will continue unabated and cause many to prophesy the ending of the world. Maitreya, however, will continue in His simple way and interpret differently these events.

Thus will Maitreya encourage men to see the marvellous breadth and scope of life, the many layers of which man knows but little till now. Gently He will introduce them bit by bit to the basic truths of our existence, the Laws which govern it, and the benefits achieved by living within these Laws. He will acquaint man with the vastness of our Galaxy and show that, in time, men of Earth will conquer Space and Time. He will encourage men to seek within, as well as without, for the answers to their problems, and validate their constant connection to each other and to Cosmos. He will remind humanity of its long history and of the many perils which man has overcome. He will sow the seeds of faith in our own illustrious future and vouchsafe the eternal divinity of man. He will show that the path of life, the evolutionary journey, leads unfailingly upwards as well as for ever onwards, and that to make the journey together, as brothers and sisters, is the surest way and the way most lit by joy. Look, then, for the signs of Maitreya's entrance, make it known, and uplift the hope of your brothers.

March 2007

The way to the stars

It will soon become apparent that humanity has come to an impasse through which there is no obvious pathway. The blind following of market forces has brought the nations to a standstill in their fierce battle for markets and profits.

Some tread more carefully as their economies falter, while others, especially the newly rich, soldier on, intent on even greater riches and growth. Slowly it is dawning on the more experienced that all is not well, that the future looks bleaker than it should, that the everdreaded slump may not be far-off, after all. One might almost say that a new realism is beginning to show itself.

In this situation there is only one way for the governments of the world to go – a way so new, so imponderable it would seem, that almost no thought has been given to its realization.

This new way is the cornerstone of Maitreya's advice to the nations. It is a way untried and yet so obvious in its efficacy that men will be astonished by the success of their actions when it is implemented. The way is sharing, the straightforward demonstration of the oneness of men. The principle of sharing brings into manifestation the quality of divinity. When men share they will reveal themselves as potential Gods. Nothing is so truly divine as this great gesture of Brotherhood. When men see this they will enter into a new definition of themselves and will begin the establishment of the Era of Righteousness. So will it be.

When Maitreya enters the lives of men and brings His counsel, a new chapter will open for men. They will know that they are not alone in this vast universe. They will know that there are many other worlds in which their Brothers work for them, saving them from much harm. Maitreya will inaugurate the era of contact with these their far off

Brothers, and will establish a future of mutual interaction and service. Thus will it be.

My friends, these are not idle dreams but the considered words of One who Knows. Take heart, therefore, and be prepared for this enlargement of your vision and capacity for service. Maitreya will show you that the way to the stars is a feasible journey of enlightenment. He will show that the units of the one life manifest themselves throughout Cosmos; that until now this knowledge has been withheld from men but will provide a sure path for future generations to follow.

Much depends, therefore, on men's response to Maitreya's guidance. Men have indeed the choice: to remain as men stunted in the growth of their magnificence, or to become what in Truth they are, veritable Gods. Maitreya is sure that men will respond from their hearts, and that He will guide them towards their Destiny.

April 2007

Saving the planet

When mankind realizes how serious is the ecological imbalance of their planetary home, they must take the steps so urgently needed to remedy the situation. If men were to fail to respond with sufficient resolution they would be guilty of surrendering the planet to slow but inevitable destruction. What, then, the legacy to hand on to their children? That this self-destruction should not prevail all must act together, and make the necessary sacrifices. This will entail a complete change in attitude to the integrity of the planet and what are seen as the needs of men today.

It will not be easy for some to countenance the changes needed but only by such change can the life of the planet be assured. Already, deep inroads have been made into the essential stock of trees on Earth. De-forestation has caused a growing loss of oxygen and the rise of carbon gases. This is now at a critical stage and requires immediate action.

The reality of global warming is now dawning on the minds of millions, yet, despite the overwhelming evidence some still deny the actions of men are the cause.

We, your Elder Brothers, can say with full conviction that the actions of men are responsible for eighty per cent of global warming.

Maitreya, you will find, will not be long in bringing this urgent problem to man's attention. He will face men with the alternatives: the beneficial results of action now, on the one hand, and the destruction which would ensue from doing nothing, or too little, on the other. Thus, the decision is man's alone.

When men understand this they will indeed rally to the cause. They will see that the future for their children depends on action now, and will elicit from Maitreya and His group the necessary steps to take. Maitreya will advocate a simpler form of living, one more in keeping with the reality of the planet's situation. When enough people are convinced that this is necessary there will be a growing movement to simplify throughout the planet. This will proceed with quite unusual speed, so inspired by the need for change will millions be. Thus will the gravest dangers facing planet Earth be somewhat countered. This will encourage many and boost their readiness for further changes.

Faced with the dilemma of necessary change men will come to realize the inevitability of accepting the principle of sharing. Only sharing will make these changes practical and possible. Only through sharing can the bounty of Planet Earth be successfully used. Only through sharing can this bounty be correctly husbanded. Only thus can the Planet itself live in harmony with its environment and with its inhabitants.

May 2007

Transformation

It will not come as a surprise to learn that the true number of civilian dead in Iraq has now exceeded 800,000, while wounded, to a greater or lesser degree, amount to at least one million. For how much longer can the occupying powers hide these figures from their people? It goes without saying that every effort is made by these powers to hide and diminish, for their own purposes, these appalling statistics of destruction. It is no wonder, therefore, that millions of Iraqis have fled their country. Is it surprising that soon the invasion of Iraq will be recognized as the greatest disaster of recent times: unlawful, unnecessary, and arrogant in the extreme?

While the world waits, the Americans and British seek to extricate themselves from the morass which they have created, and to do so with whatever dignity and plausibility they can muster. Certainly no triumphal banners are in order. The legacy is one of death, mayhem and abuse of power.

Meanwhile the forces of reconstruction have set to work to mend the fractured walls, physical in Iraq and psychological elsewhere. The world awaits anxiously the unknown results stemming from this unhappy episode but the hopes of many are curiously high, some would say, without true reason. Did men but know it, the whole world is bracing itself for momentous changes, which will set to rights, not only the trauma of the Middle East, but the dangers and tragedies of Earth itself.

Maitreya knocks loudly at the door. The door, soon, will open and the Lord of Love will step forward into the fray. When men see Him they will be astonished by the simplicity of His words but also by the clarity of His utterance. His wisdom will baffle and delight in equal measure, drawing to Him those who are ready to follow

Him and rebuild the world. His name is Valour; likewise Strength of Purpose. The Great Lord comes equipped as none before have been, ready to do battle with all that ails and belittles man.

There are many who smile at the notion of such a Presence among us, but soon all will come to know the truth of these words, and take their stand for or against Him. Thus will the Great Lord place before mankind the question of its survival. He will show that essentially men are one, no matter the colour or the creed, that the bounty of Earth belongs to all and that sharing of that bounty is the key to man's future. Only sharing, and the justice which it will bring, offers hope to man. Only justice wrought of sharing will end the plagues of war and terror. Only sharing and justice can bring men to that Brotherhood which is their true inheritance. When men see this they will rise to the challenge and tackle one by one the many problems which daunt us now.

Maitreya's Light will support and balance men in their eagerness for the changes which must ensue, and, in right order, the world will be renewed. Thus will it be.

June 2007

The turning of the wheel

When men realize how close to self destruction they have come, they will shudder to think of the consequences of their actions. Seldom has there been a time when men faced such danger. Even in the worst adversity they have fought and tested themselves against fate. In recent times, however, men have so lost a sense of their direction that they have seemed oblivious to the danger facing them. That this danger and trial are largely of their own making is no doubt responsible for their equanimity and apparent indifference. When men know this, they will be astonished to learn how close to annihilation have their actions brought them. They have indeed diced with death, putting an inconceivable strain on Those Who are pledged to help them. Men, of course, know little or nothing of this escape, and continue blithely on their path. That this path leads only to a desert wasteland they have yet to understand, so steeped are they in materialistic ambition.

Great are the possibilities which await men's creative efforts, however, and great will be their achievements when the light dawns and the blinkers drop from their eyes.

This realization will come when men turn inwards again, and find within their hearts the brotherhood and unity which all instinctively crave. Then will come the blossoming of new hope and inspiration, leading men to renew their upward climb, and to the creation of a better world. Simplicity and honest effort will replace the present corruption which stains every aspect of men's lives today. Men will seek to emulate Maitreya and His group of Masters, and so purify their structures and standards.

With Maitreya and His group to guide them, men will grow to love the simplicity of the new structures, and in them find a deep satisfaction and coherence. They will feel at ease in a world shorn of competition and the tension which it brings. Working together in co-operation they will find a profound happiness and fulfilment in all that they do.

Maitreya will stint nothing of His help and advice, nor shall We, your Elder Brothers, in Our efforts to inspire the building of the new civilization. The wonders which will grace this coming edifice will delight and astonish all men. Each will have a part to play in its construction and all will give of their best in its achievement. Thus will it be.

July 2007

Man's divinity

Deep in the consciousness of all men is the awareness of the divine. With some, it is nearer the surface of the mind; in others it lies relatively unknown and undiscovered until some major event or stimulus awakens it from sleep. Thus some affirm readily the existence of the divine while many reject, often heatedly, the reality of all that cannot be known, measured and understood by their five senses.

Today, many are sensing, more and more, the presence of Maitreya, Whose energies penetrate all the planes of consciousness. They may know not the name, or even of His existence, but, responding to His energy, are aware of a new and spiritual climate in the world. They find it difficult to explain but know with growing certainty that they live in the aura of the divine, and that all will be well. They know, too, that they are not alone, that their prayers are being answered, and that something wonderful and sacred is happening on planet Earth. They sense that the stressful and dangerous conditions of today are nearing their end, that beyond the fear and failures of our time is a new and better world to be fashioned and that it will be so fashioned.

Meanwhile, Maitreya prepares to engage with all that hinders man's progress and well-being, with all that prevents the expression of his divinity, and also with man's own fear and frailty.

He will show that man has come from the highest source and is equipped with all the potential of Gods; that, freed from the fear which holds him in thrall, man can build a civilization worthy of his divinity and creative genius.

He will show that fear and lack of trust alone condemn men to the present dangerous conditions which threaten their existence; that the simple act of sharing will bring justice and peace to their troubled world; that men must recognize themselves as one, one group, sons of the one Father.

Thus will He speak. Thus will He call on men to change.

How will men respond? How will they find Maitreya's analysis of their position and problems? Maitreya is not alone in urging change and reform in the world. Many wise men and women are responding to His thoughts and energy and propound, widely, His ideas. Slowly but surely, these ideas are taking root, and educating large masses of hitherto uninterested and uncommitted people. Thus is Maitreya's way being prepared.

Even so, how can Maitreya touch the hearts of the millions needed to change direction? The answer lies in the potency of His energies. Never before has a Teacher of such power stood before the world. With each word uttered, His beneficent force flows from heart to heart. Useless and unnecessary is argument and debate. His Truth calls forth the Truth in the heart of the listener, and in the crucible of their shared divinity is recognized as Truth Itself.

September 2007

Step by step

From time to time, We, your Elder Brothers, attempt to engage humanity in an understanding of the evolutionary process in which all are immersed, knowingly or not. To this end, We convey to disciples, in whole or in part, that Teaching which We adjudge to be of value, at that particular time, in broadening the minds of men and acquainting them with the knowledge which will lighten their journey.

From now on, while this method of teaching will continue, Maitreya and His Group will involve Themselves more and more directly with the general public. Thus humanity will see more clearly, and appreciate more completely, the connection between the Teaching, more or less esoteric in nature, of the evolutionary process and the circumstances of their lives, from moment to moment. A deeper understanding of the meaning and purpose of their lives, and of the great Laws which govern them, will in this way be established. A great step forward by humanity as a whole can thus be expected.

For disciples and initiates, the Teaching will go forward in the usual way: during the hours of sleep, and that conveyed and published through certain disciples. With this exception: since the Masters will work openly, more and more of the Teaching will come directly from Them. This, of course, will speed the process of learning, and shorten the journey for disciples to a significant degree. Furthermore, the presence of the Masters will help to obliterate the gulf which now exists between the disciples and the world of 'ordinary' men. More or less all, on one level or another, will be engaged in a conscious journey of discovery and growing awareness of the magnitude of life. Thus will it be. So far, a blueprint, only, exists for this considerable shift in emphasis of the Teaching methods used by Us, but gradually this blueprint will change into a living form from which all will benefit and grow.

Maitreya will show men that every step they take to remake their world, and to establish right human relations, is a forward step on their journey to perfection. That the inner step for the disciple must be matched by the outer step of the man not yet engaged in the initiatory process. That all is an interrelated and integrated whole. Step by step, man makes his path at his own pace; step by step, man moves from ignorance to knowledge, from injustice to justice, from slavery to freedom.

In all such endeavours, there will be times when progress seems slow and unlikely; but man will grow in confidence and trust, and learn the method of 'step by step'. His innate divinity, lost now in materialism and commercialization, will blossom anew under the teaching of Maitreya and His Group. Man will come to know himself as the creative source of all his needs.

1 September 2007
SI October 2007

*[Editor's note: From October 2007 **Share International** magazine began to include the date each article was dictated by Benjamin Creme's Master. Hereafter both dates are given.]*

The Earth in travail

It may be said that at last some men are beginning to take seriously the dangers posed by global warming and the consequent climate changes that this is bringing about. It is true that there is much disagreement over the reality and extent of the dangers, and of the best means of approaching the problems which are agreed to exist. However, there is no doubt that some men, at least, are recognizing that men face a formidable task in halting the progress of destruction and in stabilizing the environment. It is also true that even the most aware and concerned of men know little of the extent and complexity of the problems.

The problem of pollution is such a case. Pollution takes many forms, some obvious and easily dealt with, if the will to do so exists. Some, however, require a science and a remedy as yet unknown to man; they are so toxic and destructive that they must be given high priority to overcome. The effect of pollution on the quality of air, food, on animals, and on fish, in rivers and the oceans, is known but largely ignored. The most destructive of all, that caused by nuclear radiation, awaits discovery by Earth scientists. The upper levels of nuclear radiation are beyond the present atomic technology. They are also the most toxic and hazardous to man and the lower kingdoms. On all those levels the problems of pollution must be overcome. This can be achieved only by a complete reconstruction of the present political, economic and social structures.

Man has ravaged and polluted the Earth, and severely damaged his own environment. Now man must see it as a top priority to remedy what he has hurt and so restore to health his ailing planet. He must learn to simplify his demands on the planet and learn the beauty of simplicity and the joy of sharing.

Man has but little choice: the urgency of the task demands immediate action; few indeed realize the true scale of damage already done. The question may be asked: can planet Earth be saved and by what means?

The answer is a resounding YES! and by means which involve the transformation of the present modes of living by the majority of men.

The paramount ambition of all so-called 'developed' countries is to achieve an ever higher percentage of growth of their economies to become, thereby, richer; and, in an economic world based on competition, to attain dominance and power, and so enjoy a higher standard of life. This being so, the pillaging of the Earth, the cavalier waste of resources, is seen as only natural and necessary. This irresponsible action has at last brought planet Earth almost to its knees.

Maitreya, you can be sure, will not be long in addressing this urgent problem and in presenting His solutions. The first step, He will advocate, is the acceptance of the urgency which many today deny. Sharing, He will say, is the beginning of the process of change which will provide the answers to our woes and the rehabilitation of Earth.

14 October 2007
SI November 2007

Preparing the future

Towards the end of an Age and the beginning of a new Cosmic cycle, everything begins to fall apart. The old and tried ways of living no longer work, or meet the needs of an advancing humanity. Certainty gives way to uncertainty, the known has lost its power to convince, and men feel bewildered, lost and filled with fear. Thus is it today as we stand, baffled, in this transitional phase between the old Age of Pisces and the new Aquarian dispensation.

The Aquarian Age will last approximately 2,350 years and will bring much benefit to men as its energies mount in potency over the centuries. However, at present, the old ways of Pisces, outworn but not as yet outgrown, still hold sway and determine the thoughts and actions of the majority of men. This being so, countless millions are held in thrall by the actions of those leaders whose nations are powerful and dominant at the present time. Thus is this a time of upheaval and stress, disharmony and strife.

That this troubled time will not last much longer you may be assured. Already, the signs of change are evident to Us, your Elder Brothers. We see clearly the outlines of conditions altogether different from those that now prevail. We see a world at peace, a world where justice reigns, where freedom adorns the lives of men and women everywhere. We know that the present ills are transient and passing, that the time is not far off for the light of the New Dawn to illumine men's lives and challenge them to action. We know also that men in their hearts are ready and longing for change, and will rise to the challenge with eagerness and will; they await only inspiration and guidance.

That inspiration and guidance Maitreya is eager to bestow, in full measure and more, as He awaits the appointed hour which, by karmic law, allows Him to proceed.

Then will the Great Lord enter, openly, the domain of men. Then will He challenge the assumptions of the men of power and wealth. Maitreya will speak for the millions without a voice; for the destitute and hungry who live in anguish from day to day; for those who languish in the prisons of the world for daring to challenge the edicts of their 'betters'. He will speak for all men who love justice and liberty and will raise His voice aloud in their cause. He will temper the wrath of those who govern by war; He will seal for ever the door through which war enters and defiles the realm of man. All this, through men, He will accomplish, and so restore sanity and peace to Earth.

Calmly, and with purpose, He prepares the golden future, the inheritance of men, and gathers together the 'shining lights', the men and women who will fashion that future.

11 November 2007
SI December 2007

A call to the media

For many years men have awaited, impatiently to be sure, evidence that Maitreya does in truth exist, and carries out His work among us. Why this doubt should for so long persist is, perhaps, difficult to understand, given the vast transformations of our world which have clearly taken place, each one foretold by Maitreya, and made available to the public and world media. What prevents the acceptance – even as a hypothesis – that such a welcome event has indeed transpired?

The media of the world know every facet of this information, however little they inform the public of its nature. Many of its representatives have met Maitreya, have heard Him speak, and yet stay silent themselves.

Why should this be so? What inhibits the public announcement of this welcome news? In the main the problem is fear: fear of ridicule, fear of disbelief; fear of loss, of their status or jobs; fear that they are somehow beguiled, that they did not see what they saw or hear what they heard. It is easier to set their experiences aside and to leave it to Maitreya Himself – if He does indeed exist – to come forward and show the world His factual Presence.

This view, logical enough to those who thus wait silently, shows little understanding of the Laws which govern the appearance of a Teacher of Maitreya's stature.

Many worthy Teachers come into our lives, do their work, and cause few ripples on the surface of men's thought and action. They seldom need forerunners to prepare their way. Maitreya, however, is the World Teacher, Head of Hierarchy, and intends to serve as such for the next world cycle. His impact on humanity cannot be comprehended. His coming is a truly momentous happening, which must be prepared for beforehand, and adequately explained to men of every station.

The world's media are ideally placed to acquaint men with the true happenings of our time. They are looked to for information, and often guidance, by millions of people thirsty for the truth, for knowledge and hope. It behoves the men and women of the media, men and women of goodwill, to acquaint *themselves* with this information, where necessary, and to serve the public by its serious introduction. Then will they see Maitreya openly, ready to show us all how to set to rights the world.

12 January 2008
SI January/February 2008

The Christ as Teacher

Many people await and expect the emergence of the Christ but hold a very distorted view of how that will affect humanity. Many await Him as a Spiritual Magician Who will cancel out their and others' shortcomings, and so establish everlasting peace. Theirs is a very passive view of this vast and complex happening. For Maitreya, Himself, it is an opportunity to come into a dynamic interaction with humanity, to establish the Principles of the Divine Plan, and to inaugurate the era of Right Human Relationship.

This entails the active response and participation of men and women everywhere: a worldwide, continuous process of change in outer structures and inner perceptions.

Maitreya does not see as particularly open and fruitful those areas of the world where Christians are in the majority. Nor do other major religions inspire in Him more hope of understanding. To be sure, in all religions are men and women who are ready to respond and to act for the benefit of all. Likewise, in every walk of life, in every country in the world, people await the signal that will summon them to action on behalf of their brothers and sisters, known and unknown.

Many await the Christ as the Judge, sent to chasten and punish the lawbreakers. Maitreya, the Christ, is a Teacher, and will indeed teach man the Laws of Life, but a Judge He never was, nor does punishment hold a place in His vocabulary. He will seek to inspire men to know themselves as souls in incarnation, travelling a journey of self-discovery together, and helping each other along the way. He will affirm that competition hinders and deflects men from their path, rendering sterile each glimpse of the soul's nature.

Men have strayed far from that Path. Commercialization has humanity by the throat and is squeezing every generous thought and gesture out of their lives. The souls of men can endure little more of this oppression and are crying aloud in their agony and frustration. They wonder, then, at the upsurge of crime and mayhem committed by the young in every land.

Maitreya will acquaint men with the origin of wars and military action around the world. He will show how even the climate and weather are disaffected as a result. Men have much to learn about the effects of their actions, and the need for discipline and care.

The Christ comes to teach. Men, free will intact, must respond in order to grow. The Christ, Maitreya, never uses force, even if thus we would the sooner learn. He knows that only that which is undertaken by man's free will is lawful and likely to bear fruit.

10 February 2008
SI March 2008

The people awaken

It may seem impossible to believe, or so much wishful thinking, but from the higher viewpoint of your Elder Brothers, significant changes for the better are taking place throughout the world. We see a growing movement towards unity and justice, and a growing realization of the absolute necessity for peace to reign if humanity is to continue on its path of evolution. This represents a huge step back from the brink of self-destruction.

There are many, of course, who still conceive and perfect the tools of war, waxing rich and powerful in this deadly trade. The people, however, are awakening; a different drum is beating a new rhythm and the peoples respond. In almost every country men are sensing a new light, a quickening thought, a rising hope. Freedom, Justice and Peace are beginning to be felt as nearer, more real, more possible of attainment than ever before. Global communications are giving men a new sense of themselves as one humanity. This new awareness is not complete or perfect, to be sure, but We see clearly the beginning of a new and hopeful trend in this direction. This, indeed, gladdens Our hearts and betokens correct response to the energies of the New Time.

When Maitreya steps forward and begins His open Mission, this trend will magnify and become the aim and purpose of men and women of goodwill in every country. More and more, men will understand that, despite the differences in colour, race and religion, men and women everywhere are one, that they require the same justice and freedom which some believe is theirs alone by right.

Maitreya will emphasize the utter necessity for peace, and that the complete renunciation of war can only be achieved by trust. Sharing alone, Maitreya will affirm, can engender that trust.

Thus will Maitreya speak, thus will He foster the sense of the One humanity and the need for sharing. Needless to say, not all men will respond to Maitreya's call for Unity and Brotherhood, but as the voice of reason and justice penetrates the hearts of men, more and yet more will see the truth of His insight and the necessity for change. Thus will it be, and thus will men awaken to the Light of Truth that is among them, and will see Him as their Leader and Guide. Gently, yet firmly, He will coax men to act in their own highest interests. Like an elder brother He will lead the younger members of His family step by step towards their own truth.

This time is not far off, in truth is very near. Watch and listen for the rising voice of the peoples of the world as hope and joy alike arise in their hearts.

Then will you know that the wheel has turned. That the pain of poverty and injustice will be no more. That the blasphemy of war is renounced for ever. That the Law of Love has found its rightful place in the hearts of men and women everywhere in this, our world.

9 March 2008
SI April 2008

The cities of tomorrow

If and when a man of Mars lands his spacecraft on Earth and looks around him, he must surely be amazed by his surroundings. Unless his mission has taken him to the countryside, he will wonder how the people of Earth can tolerate the abject monotony and raw ugliness of so many towns and cities of the world. The teeming squalor of the poorest is matched only by the brash, arid rawness of the richest. Wherever one looks on Earth, it would seem, office blocks like gigantic ants' nests cover the ground, surrounded by endless rows of near identical cubes in which the exhausted ants recover in sleep. Of course, our friend from Mars would discover, there are exceptions to this ubiquitous life-denying mediocrity, but, he will find, they are all relics of the past, proudly maintained and preserved as tourists' pleasure grounds while the local population make do in silent envy.

The above is, of course, a caricature, but it is not for nothing that among Maitreya's priorities is the beautification of our cities. A city is more than just a place where money can be made and the fruits of the making enjoyed. It is a Centre, a Magnet which draws groups of people together to heighten and enrich the consciousness of all. It is a place in which the soul of the country which it graces can manifest and adorn the achievements of men everywhere. A city, therefore, should be a place of beauty, of great variety and colour, with many quiet areas for meditation and rest. It should not be too big; many modern cities repel rather than attract their citizens. They should be open and welcoming to all, sharing their special gifts with local and visitor alike.

A city is a charged centre of energy, each one different and expressing many different rays or qualities. Together, they fashion the personality of a country and provide the opportunity for the soul of the nation to be expressed. When Maitreya and the Masters are working openly the importance of certain cities will become clearer.

As great centres of population, the coming science of energy will naturally blossom in cities. The new Science of Light will transform the outer appearance of all cities in the world. The energy of light, direct from the sun, will flow into and from containers of various size while the Power of Shape will determine the nature of the energy needed and stored.

It will, no doubt, take many years to transform the cities of today into the places of beauty which they will become. However, men need to be able to visualize that such cities can and will be built, and existing cities slowly rebuilt. As the population of Earth decreases, as it will, cities will reach their ultimate best size and flourish.

12 April 2008
SI May 2008

As men look back

A few years from now, looking back, men will wonder why they hesitated so long in taking the obvious and most natural action: sharing the resources of the world. Experiencing warmly the new stability, the lack of tension, the ease of international co-operation, men will wonder how they could have been so blind to the self-evident, so wilful and destructive to their own best interests for so long.

Humanity stands now at the threshold of an entirely new experience in which every global decision and act will be seen to be for the better, as nourishing and sanctifying their lives, and strengthening the bonds of Brotherhood which, up till then, they had ignored and all but forgotten. Gladly, men will now work together for the Common Good, the hatred and distrust of the past put firmly behind them. Thus will a new kinship emerge as Goodwill and Respect, like vitalizing yeast, saturate their awakened lives. Thus, too, in ever strengthening measure, will love and joy embrace and lighten the hearts of men and women everywhere.

What subtle alchemy can it be that will work this magical transformation in the lives of men? Not alchemy but the divinity which dwells in the hearts of men themselves, evoked and brought forth by the wonder of Maitreya's Love. "Sharing," He has said, "is divine; the first step into sharing is the first step into your divinity." In man himself lies the full measure of that divinity. Sharing will demonstrate that man is a potential God and is equipped to express the creative Will of his Source.

Slowly but surely, that creative Purpose will manifest through men and so direct their actions and decisions. The old lawlessness will wither away and disappear like a faded memory of a distant, childish past. So will it be.

We, your elder Brothers, see ever more clearly the outlines of a brilliant future stretching ahead for men; We see the blueprints of a science which would astonish the most fertile and sophisticated minds of today; We see, too, an art whose beauty and creative power has never, as yet, been seen by men.

Above all, We recognize that this creative outflow, unprecedented in scope in human history, is the inevitable result of the great inner change through which humanity is passing: learning to live within the Laws of Life. When men see and understand this consciously, as a fact of life, they will take, gladly, the steps which lead directly to Peace and Justice, Freedom and Right Relationship. That first step is called Sharing.

With Maitreya, the Lord of Love, and His group of Masters to help and guide, how can men fail to see that Sharing and Right Relationship are the same, have the same impulse: to demonstrate the urge to Unity which underlies our apparent separation, and so reveal the true nature of men as Gods.

23 April 2008
SI June 2008

The Oneness of Humanity

The time is soon coming when men will see for themselves that the direction on which they are now embarked is false, fruitless for their future happiness, and doomed to failure. Seeing this, they will pose the questions: Why this emptiness? Why do we fail to achieve the peace we seek? Where have we gone wrong? Turning then to Maitreya, they will evaluate His words, testing them for relevance to their plight. They will find that central to Maitreya's thought is the concept of Oneness. Men must, He will assure them, see themselves as One, each part of a united Whole – the human family – and that all that they do must reflect that Oneness. The present failure to appreciate this reality, He will contend, is responsible for all our difficulties and troubles, our disharmony and fears, our conflicts and wars.

"See your brother as yourself," says Maitreya. Create an International Storehouse from which all can take. Only thus, by Sharing, can the world be renewed, is His Teaching. Only by Sharing, He will affirm, will men find the happiness they seek. Sharing alone will bring Justice and Peace.

Thus will Maitreya guide the thoughts of men towards the Truth that He brings and is. Thus will Maitreya show men their errors and the solution to their dilemma, and thus will men take stock of their situation and, in growing numbers, realize the Truth of His advice. More and more, men will see that Maitreya's guidance is the only way to achieve the happiness and peace all inwardly crave. Held back by fear until then, they will find in His simple Teaching the answer to all their fears and woes.

Naturally, not all will find in Maitreya the guide they seek. Many, indeed, will find in His Teaching, all that they fear and hate. Gradually, however, the ardour of those who can respond and resonate to His simple words of Truth will bring millions to His cause of Justice and Peace. His Teaching, though simple, will penetrate the hearts of all those in whom love has not yet been extinguished.

Thus will Maitreya work throughout the world, drawing to His side all who long for a new start, a simpler, happier world wherein to raise their families in peace and harmony.

The Day of Declaration will be the signal for that new start for Planet Earth. On that day without precedent, men will experience the Oneness of which Maitreya speaks. They will sense that all humanity is undergoing the same experience. They will feel a humble pride in being one of a huge family of brothers and sisters whose hearts are beating together in a love altogether new. This sense of belonging together will embrace them and bring tears of long-forgotten joy to each and every one.

15 June 2008
SI July/August 2008

See Him and rejoice

Many times over the years have I said that Maitreya was emerging 'soon', and thus has this expectation been kept vividly alive in the hearts of millions. That His full emergence has not yet taken place is not a sign of perfidy on My part, but rather a result of the extraordinary nature and difficulty of this enterprise. Men in general know nothing of the laws which govern such an event, nor of the boundaries to Maitreya's action which these laws create.

Also, We, your Elder Brothers, work outside and beyond the notion of time, and find difficulty in placing Our insights and information before men whose understanding is still governed by the 'fact' of time. Nevertheless, when all is said, this present 'time' should be seen by men as the anteroom in which Maitreya patiently awaits the signal to emerge openly onto the world stage. The present chaotic conditions, especially in the economic and financial fields, have tipped the scales and made possible a decision on a period which men themselves would welcome as 'soon'. It will not be long, therefore, until the Great Lord begins His open mission, albeit undeclared. Watch and wait with a sure understanding of His priorities, and so miss Him not.

How will humanity view this extraordinary man, like none seen in recent memory yet obviously one of us? How will men respond to the simple truth of His utterance? And how quickly will men respond to His analysis of their plight? It is not possible to know precisely how men will react on first experience of Maitreya. The Great Lord will be circumspect and relatively restrained on first appearance, lest He drive away those who need time to evaluate His thoughts and judge their relevance. Soon, however, many We surmise will gather round Him, eager to see adopted the changes He advises. They, in their turn, will stir their brothers and sisters to consider these seminal ideas, and to launch a crusade for sanity in world affairs. These ideas, requiring a complete reconstruction of our present way of life, will gradually appear more logical, more practical and achievable than first they may have seemed, and so a great wave of enthusiasm for sharing and right relationship will sweep across the world. Maitreya, Himself, will potentize these natural stirrings of right thinking among the nations, and will work to foster the growing public yearning for a new direction.

Thus will Maitreya work through men to sow the seeds of the New Garden. Thus will He engender in men a longing for the real and the true, for the manifestation of love and justice. In this way does the Great Lord serve humanity, showing them the way to live within the Spiritual Laws. Thus will the Lord of Love reveal Himself to men: as a Brother, a Friend, a Way-shower, a Traveller, like them, on the Way.

See Him soon then and rejoice; join His ranks and serve; awaken through Him to your divinity.

14 July 2008
SI September 2008

Man's destiny

When men awaken to their true potential they will be amazed by the range of creativity which will become theirs. The audacity of their thought will at first astound them, and will lead them into enterprises all but unimaginable today. Men will find that they are, in truth, potential Gods. From the deep slumber of the past men will awaken and slough off the heavy coat of ignorance which for long has delayed their forward progress. Thus will it be.

Man is now at the turning point in his long adventure in life on planet Earth. From now on, all progress will be the result of his considered will and reason. No longer will greed and competition impede his journey to perfection; no longer will war, and want for millions, degrade and stain his path; never again will lawlessness and separation rule on planet Earth.

Man's foot now stands on a ladder of ascent which will take him to the very stars.

As We, your elder Brothers, take Our places beside you, you will see in Us exemplars, and be inspired to become like Us. You will see that We know no competition, that We value all life in whatever form. You will see that We love without distinction or condition; and work only and always for the fulfilment of the Plan. Men are destined by the Plan to reach that same perfection; Ours is the task to show them the way.

The path to such perfection is well trodden by Us and We have set in place the needed landmarks: men must see humanity as One, brothers and sisters, sons of the One Father.

Freedom and Justice are essential to all, everywhere, without exception, and can only be achieved by trust.

Sharing alone can create that trust, and set men on the path to their divinity.

Men, to be happy, must live within the Laws of Life: of Cause and Effect, Rebirth, Harmlessness and Sacrifice. These basic Laws are the Ancient Landmarks which protect men from self-destruction and remorse.

When Maitreya steps forward into open vision you will hear these Laws again, for they form the basis of all His teaching and the basis of all life on planet Earth.

The awakening of men depends on humanity grasping the import of these Laws and their willingness and readiness to change. This present so-called civilization has 'shot its bolt', is decayed and dying, with little further to offer men than hardship and fear, and, finally, self-annihilation.

Maitreya comes to show men that they have within themselves all that it takes to become the Gods they essentially are. To show them how simple and beautiful is that way, and to inspire them to grasp and accept their destiny. Maitreya doubts not their response.

5 September 2008
SI October 2008

The stage is set

For many years We, your Elder Brothers, have warned men of the dangers of blindly following market forces which, themselves, are blind. Thus, the present widespread economic and financial crisis should not be unexpected. The 'bubble' created by competition and greed had, inevitably, to burst. Yet the 'men of money' who built this towering edifice on shifting sands are stunned by the outcome, are at a loss to understand the reasons for the catastrophe and are already looking for better ways of continuing the same folly.

The people of the countries worst hit by the recent events, however, know well the reasons for the collapse, and are angry in the knowledge that it is they who will suffer hardship and want in the months and years ahead.

Maitreya, waiting patiently in the wings, sees this as a 'window of opportunity' which allows Him to emerge openly and begin His outer mission. Thus, the long wait for His emergence is almost over. Very soon indeed now men will hear Maitreya's call for action and for change.

Already, amid the myriad analysts the media have turned to for explanation and advice in the current crisis are a few who wisely warn that radical change is essential; that control and regulation of the 'men of money' must be a top priority to prevent a repetition. The people call for fairness and justice and are in no mood to be ignored. Thus the stage is set, at last, for the words of Maitreya to be heard, and to be seen as sensible and true. He will tell men that the continuation of the present disorder will bring only further chaos; that only a complete and ordered reconstruction of the world's economic system will bring justice and peace; that without such justice and peace the future would be bleak indeed. He will tell them that we have the answer in our hands, that the world is one; that we live and prosper as one or face annihilation. These things, bit by bit, Maitreya will tell the world and the people will respond. Before their present leaders, they will see His good sense, and welcome the opportunity to put into practice His advice.

How long this phase will last is difficult to predict but, in the present chaotic conditions it may be relatively short indeed. The greedy 'men of money' have been caught out and their methods found wanting. The people who only want sufficient to raise their families in decency are more than ready for the changes and the challenges of the future. They want justice and peace and are prepared to share to achieve these precious goals. The people are ready; the 'men of money' are bewildered and are licking their wounds; Maitreya, too, is ready, and has His hand on the door.

11 October 2008
SI November 2008

Evolution versus creationism

Many people believe, or affect to believe, that this world as it stands today is not more than 5,000 years old; that Man and all the creatures of the animal kingdom and the rocks of the mineral kingdom were created in a few days, fully fledged and finished in all aspects.

They hold that evolution is a myth, that the Christian Bible account of creation is literally true and correct. To accept such a theory it is necessary to close one's eyes to science in general and to the sciences of geology, anthropology, palaeontology and archaeology in particular.

It is indeed true to say that there was a time when men did not walk the Earth, when dinosaurs, gigantic in size, roamed and ruled instead. It is also true that, according to Our reckoning, Man's history is infinitely older than today's science believes. By today's reckoning, humanity is approximately five or six million years old at the most. By Our science and tradition, however, early animal-man had reached the point when individualization became possible, and the 'Sons of mind' began their long journey of evolution. It has taken Man 18-and-a-half million years to reach the level of today. How then is it possible for intelligent, educated 'creationists' to hold, against the evidence of science, what seems to be a ludicrous concept?

The answer lies in the fact that the evolutionists and the creationists are really arguing at cross-purposes; both, in their limited way are right. Modern scientists, looking objectively at the findings of Darwin, have accumulated a wealth of evidence for the case of evolution, a long, slow development of men from animal ancestors, in particular by the development of mind.

The creationists look to the Christian Bible as their guide, ignoring the fact that the Bible was written by hundreds of people over hundreds of years; that it is written in symbolic language, and is meant to be symbolic rather than factual. The creationist is at pains to emphasise that 'Man' was made by God, in 'God's own image', and so owes nothing to evolution. To such, Darwin and those who follow him are missing the point about Man: that he is a spiritual being, of divine heritage, and if he does not always behave as God's creation he has been corrupted by Satan.

Can these two diametrically opposed views be bridged and expanded at the same time? From Our point of understanding the scientists of today, the evolutionists, are undoubtedly correct in their analysis of Man's development from the animal kingdom. We owe our physical bodies to the animal kingdom. That, however, does not make us animals. Darwin, and those who correctly followed his thought, describes only the outer, physical development of Man, largely ignoring that we are all engaged in the development of consciousness. The human body has all but reached its completeness: there remains little further to be achieved. From the standpoint of consciousness, however, man has scarcely taken the first steps towards a flowering which will prove that man is indeed divine, a Soul in incarnation. One day, the fact of the Soul will be proved by science and so become generally accepted, and the old dichotomy will be healed.

9 November 2008
SI December 2008

Maitreya's first interview

In the very near future, people everywhere will have the opportunity to witness an extraordinary and significant sign, the like of which has been manifested only once before, at the birth of Jesus. Then, according to Christian teaching, a star appeared in the heavens and led three wise men from the East to the birthplace of Jesus. Soon, once again, a star-like luminary of brilliant power will be seen around the world. What does this mean? How is it possible?

The answer lies in the fact that this mysterious event is a sign, and heralds the beginning of Maitreya's open mission. Soon after the sign appears in our skies, Maitreya will give His first media interview on American television.

On that open, public occasion, still unannounced as Maitreya, the World Teacher will present His views on the economic and financial chaos which now grips the world. He will explain its origins and final outcome, and present, to some extent, His recipe for amelioration of the present heavy burden on the poor of the world. Thus He will prepare the way for a more detailed and specific announcement of His ideas.

How will viewers respond? They will not know His background or status. Will they listen to and consider His words? It is too soon to know exactly but the following may be said: Never before will they have seen or heard Maitreya speak. Nor, while listening, will they have experienced His unique energy, heart to heart. Also, this is a unique time in history with whole nations stunned and apprehensive for the future. Therefore it can be assumed that many who hear His words will be open and eager to hear more. It is not for nothing that Maitreya has waited patiently for this moment to enter the public world; America, for one, would not have responded sooner. Now, for the first time in many years, a new Administration has to cope with financial chaos, unemployment and social unrest on a massive scale. The moment of truth for America and the world has arrived.

Not alone in America but worldwide, people are awakening to the need for and the possibility of change. The politicians and economists call the present situation a 'downturn' and a 'recession'. In truth, we are witnessing the last stumbling steps of the old order. Millions are becoming aware that unbridled competition and greed are not the safest path for men, that such materialistic doctrines create a 'slippery slope' for the unwary, and, eventually, the international crisis we have today.

Of course, many people of burgeoning wealth stand clear of the present loss of confidence in the ways which have made them rich, and think it only 'a matter of time' until we are back on course and thriving again.

Will they heed Maitreya and recognize the sense of His argument? Lost in their arrogance and self-esteem, possibly not. However, many are less sanguine about a return to the status quo. Many have suffered painful losses and have lost faith in the old methods. The peoples of the nations are ripe and ready for change. They call out for change and a more meaningful life. Maitreya will remind men of the essentials without which there is no future for man: Justice and Peace. And the only way to both is through sharing.

11 December 2008
SI January/February 2009

The moment has come

Eventually, men will realize that they are travelling together on a journey of Self-discovery, one which will bring them in time to the feet of the Most Holy.

The essence of this journey of discovery is that it is self-enacted and willed, and at the same time is shared by all members, known and unknown, of the human family. True it is that all men are brothers, sons of the One Father, each engaged, consciously or otherwise, in this momentous adventure we call life. To many today, unfortunately, this adventure is a painful and degrading experience; to millions, it is unjust and barren, the sooner over the better.

Small wonder is it, therefore, that so many see life as drudgery and grind, their child-engendered dreams of achievement and happiness but distant memories.

Men are born to create and grow in Self-awareness, and need the environment in which that becomes possible. The terrible disease of commercialization has robbed countless millions of their birthright and, as its insidious growth encroaches on all aspects of men's lives, its tentacles of disaster squeeze every generous and human feeling from their hearts. Humanity is in thrall to commercialization and in peril of its soul.

What can men do to reverse this process of disaster? Already, the current economic and financial chaos, symptoms of the destructive forces of commercialization, are showing men that they can no longer allow this monster to rule their lives; that they must take stock and assess anew their priorities for a more just and healthy economic structure which will the better serve their needs.

There are, of course, many, relatively untouched by the current crisis, who see this time as a 'downturn' and look forward in full confidence to the inevitable 'upturn', when we can carry on as before. This is no longer possible; the blind can no longer lead the blind. They know not of Maitreya.

Maitreya has chosen this moment to fulfil His promise to enter the domain of men and to help them on their journey. He is emerging now; His herald, the star-sign of His emergence, is seen worldwide by many and is the signal of His appearance, openly, before men. Using the television resources of today, He will engage on a series of interviews starting in America and including Japan and many other countries.

As an ordinary man, undeclared as Maitreya, He will speak for all those who have no voice, no spokesman. He will call on men to share the goods of the Earth and to embrace each other as the brothers and sisters they are. He will show that if we would have peace there is only one way to achieve it: that is by the realization of justice throughout the world, and that justice can only be achieved through sharing. We await the response of all men and women of goodwill in this, our world.

8 February 2009
SI March 2009

The restoration of the world

From almost every point of view the situation facing men everywhere grows daily more painful. The economic chaos resulting from years of unlicensed greed and heartless competition lays waste the honest toil and aspiration of countless millions. On the whole, the men of money go blithely on, their treasure intact, while men and women in every country face joblessness, poverty and fear. More accurate readings of climatic changes show men how close this planet is to irreversible calamity, and alarm bells sound loudly on many political fronts, raising to new levels the factor of stress.

How much more of this tension can humanity bear? For how long will men accept, mildly, their fate? Desperate men do desperate deeds and already in their minds, if not yet in their actions, many contemplate revolution.

Behind the scenes, Maitreya watches carefully these happenings, and gives succour wherever the Law allows. He waits, patiently, for the build-up of response to the sign of His Emergence, the "star-like luminary of brilliant power" on which many now gaze in wonder and even love.

What is desired is some measure of public debate about the significance or meaning of the Star, thus signifying the emergence of Maitreya, the World Teacher. The greater and more public the discussion, the greater does it prepare the way for Maitreya's entry. Soon there will be no gainsaying. Very soon, Venus will move beyond the sight of men and so leave the platform of the heavens open to the Star. Then there will be no doubt that the Star is there for all to see.

If sufficient discussion can be fostered on the various media and internet it will not be long until men see and hear Maitreya speak. He will not be so called, that men can judge His ideas rather than His status.

As the economic crisis deepens, a singular reaction is appearing in many countries: alongside the fear, bravado and growing despair is a new understanding of the reasons for the crash — the greed and competitive spirit at the centre of our systems and, therefore, the need for sharing. Of themselves, many are awakening to this basic truth and see sharing as the answer to injustice and war. Thus are many ready for Maitreya's Call. This realization will grow as the crisis bites deeper and deeper into the shaky fabric of the outworn forms and structures that no longer work, can never be made to work for long.

When Maitreya speaks, He will show that this is so, that the world is ready for the adoption of new and better forms, based on the true needs of the peoples everywhere. His is the task to focus and strengthen this growing realization of the oneness and unity of men, of their mutual dependence and awakening divinity. Thus will Maitreya and humanity work together for the restoration of this world.

16 March 2009
SI April 2009

The curse of commercialization

If men are to save this planet from the results of global warming they must do infinitely more than is planned to limit carbon emissions, and in a shorter period of time than is generally accepted as necessary. Men have been slow to recognize the dangers, and even now many refuse to take the problems seriously. Such attitudes, there is no doubt, put in jeopardy the future of planet Earth. At most, men have ten to fifteen years in which to establish a balance before irreparable damage is done.

To achieve this goal, men must change dramatically the present way of life, and embrace simpler forms of living and working. Gone are the days in which men raped and ravaged the planet at will, without a thought for the generations still to come, neither seeing nor caring ought for the environment which has gradually and inevitably decayed.

Each year, and for many years, huge areas of ancient primal forest are cleared of life-giving trees for purely commercial benefits. Commercialization indeed bodes ill for humanity as it tightens its grip on the throats of men. Commercialization, says Maitreya, is more dangerous to men than the atomic bomb, and is showing its destructive power in the economic chaos which rules in the world today.

How long will it take governments and their peoples to see this? How long till commercialization squeezes the life-blood out of humanity, and itself withers and dies?

More and more, the truth of these words is borne in on the minds of millions who now, suddenly, are jobless and homeless and in despair.

This has produced a situation in which Maitreya can step forward into public work without infringing humanity's free will. Patiently has Maitreya waited many years for this time, sure in the knowledge that the events now taking place would, indeed, transpire. Commercialization has bared its claws and shown its power to harm. The complacency of millions is turning into hatred and distrust of commercialization and the old order of things. Men everywhere are at last ready for a new interpretation of the meaning and purpose of life, for sharing, justice and peace; for right relationship, brotherhood and greater happiness. They are ready, at last, for Maitreya's call.

Of course, not all men have undergone this change. There are many who imagine they can 'sit out' this 'recession' and rebuild their fortunes as before. The very rich and clever ones have lost nothing. The gap between themselves and others has simply widened in their favour. They fail to understand that this time is like none other. We have reached the end of the old order. Cosmic forces dictate the changes that must and will take place, otherwise life would flourish no more on planet Earth.

Those who are ready will quickly respond to Maitreya's Teaching as He puts into simple and eloquent words their heartfelt needs. Others will take longer to forgo that to which they have become accustomed, and for a time disagree. In time, millions around the world will see the need and the logic of the changes which alone will save the planet and its people.

17 April 2009
SI May 2009

Man's emerging divinity

In all history there has never been a time like the present. Never, in all the cycles which have left their mark on man's evolution, has there been the same potential for change. This time, therefore, is unique. It portends a change in consciousness so dramatic and far-reaching that new definitions and vocabulary must evolve to describe man as he will become.

The main factor in this profound event will be the influence of man's Elder Brothers, the Masters of Wisdom, led by Maitreya, the Christ and World Teacher. It is impossible to overstate the effect which Their Great Approach will have on the lives and thoughts and behaviour of men.

Many times have you heard that man is a potential God; these are not empty words but the very truth of man's nature and Being. It is a matter of time only until that truth is verified and expressed for all to see.

The Masters will give of Their Bounty of harmlessness, wisdom and love, and steer man's ship safely to the harbour of achievement. Thus will it be. In time, men will take their due places and work together with the Masters for the benefit of all. Thus will men learn the Laws of Life and Love and fashion a future of unparalleled beauty.

The second great stimulus to man's forward growth will come from far Aquarius. Already, as our sun enters more and more deeply into the field of influence of that mighty constellation, a ferment of change arises in the hearts and minds of men.

The essential quality of Aquarius is Synthesis, a quality rarely seen in today's life on Earth. However, in gathering momentum, the quality of Synthesis will gradually replace, in all departments of life, the fragmentation and disharmony of today. Men will come to understand the meaning of Unity, and to recognize that they are brothers and sisters of one family journeying together on a voyage of discovery.

When men look back to this time they will see it as a stepping-stone to Grace. Today's chaotic turmoil is nothing less. From this turmoil will emerge the new forms which will grace the new civilization – new and better forms which will provide for men everywhere, and gratify the hearts of everyone.

Man, himself, is undergoing such stimuli that he may well feel nervous of the future.

He sees and understands little of the enormous changes which are already under way and clings vainly to the past. Soon, this fear and nervousness will be replaced by courage and commitment to the work of transformation. Under the guidance of Maitreya and His Group men will lay the cornerstones of the new and better life of which, in their various ways, all men dream.

24 April 2009
SI June 2009

The time of revelation

For many years, the peoples of most countries have followed, more or less meekly, the edicts of their legislators, the politicians. This has largely been the case whether the legislative system was democratic or otherwise. This is now beginning to change. Far from quiet acceptance of unpopular laws, peoples in many countries now demonstrate and demand change. With the exception of those countries under tight military rule, the people, more and more, are demanding to be heard, to have their needs addressed, and bad laws righted. As the beneficent energies of Aquarius gain in potency, this growing power of the people will multiply and become the most powerful voice on Earth. So much is this the case, even now, that governments of all kinds are forced to take account of the peoples' reaction to laws which deeply concern their welfare. It becomes increasingly difficult for governments to govern along strictly factional lines. Much government action is secretive and obscure, much is done 'behind the scenes' of which the people never hear, but generally, governments, at least in the so-called 'democratic' world, are careful not to rouse the ire or discontent of the people.

There is one major area in which this is assuredly not the case. For over sixty years, governments worldwide have withheld from the people the reality of 'UFOs' or 'flying saucers'. Further, they have sought by all means to denigrate the occupants of these visiting craft as 'aliens', destructive and harmful to the people of Earth. To keep their populations under control, and to avoid 'panic', they have denied the experience of hundreds of thousands of intelligent, open-minded citizens. They have thus created a major myth: "'flying saucers' do not exist but they are dangerous and rapacious to men of Earth"! Likewise, they have taught the people to deride the notion that crop circles are a legacy from Space, yet every government has unassailable proof of the existence, creativity and superior technology of these brave and harmless visitors from the sister planets of our System. Our profound ignorance of the subtle planes of matter has allowed the major governments of the world to maintain this deception for so long.

At last the time of revelation has arrived. For no longer will government agencies hide the truth from men of Earth: their brotherhood with the far-off planets of our Solar System. Already, the "star-like luminary", the Herald of Maitreya's emergence, is showing people worldwide that for years they have been deceived by their governments. You may be sure that Maitreya will reveal the truth of our relationship with the other planets, and of the co-operation which for long has continued between us. It is in truth the time of revelation.

14 June 2009
SI July/August 2009

The blasphemy of war

Twice, last century, the world was convulsed by total war, two terrible phases of one war which cost humanity many millions of lives. Each was meant to be "the war to end war", but still there are those who plot and plan for yet another trial of strength, with weapons of even greater destructiveness. How long, we must ask, will it take man to realize that war solves nothing, proves nothing and adds only pain and loss to the peoples of Earth?

A major reason for the Masters' return to the everyday world is, precisely, to remind men of this, to so influence their thinking that they turn away from war for ever. So many nations today possess the nuclear bomb, the most destructive weapon ever conceived and built, that a future major war would be the ultimate horror: the complete destruction of life on planet Earth. For many millions of years Earth would be a dead planet, a toxic waste. Men, themselves, would have to incarnate on some dark, far-off world, and begin again the long, long journey into the light.

You may be sure that when Maitreya, imminently, begins His open mission, He will face men with this problem and its outcome, and offer His solution and advice. War, He will remind men, is a blasphemy, a detestation and crime against all men, involved or not. War, He will say, must be considered thus if humanity and the lower kingdoms are to survive.

Sharing and justice alone, He will say, will ensure the future for men. Strive for unity and co-operation for the men of Earth are One. "See your brother as yourself" and take the first step into your divinity. "Take your brother's need as the measure for your action and solve the problems of the world. There is no other course."

Thus will Maitreya speak to the people of Earth. Thus will He endeavour to change the direction of their thinking.

Will the people listen to and act on His advice? Fear and foreboding fill the minds of men: ancient habits of thought die hard and are loath to change.

More and more, however, the problems and privations which accompany the economic collapse of today encourage men to seek new ways of living, and turn their thoughts to sharing, to the creation of a more just and generous world. Thus are many ready to respond to Maitreya's words. Many, of course, are not ready to change. Many are content with the present situation, expecting an 'upturn' in the markets before too long, when they will begin again to make money from air for their company and themselves.

Many, too, in the religious fields, will welcome little the appearance of Maitreya. Bereft of knowledge, clinging to their man-made dogmas, they will find in Maitreya, the Lord of Love, the abomination of evil that they fear. But not all. Many religious groups around the world have seen and heard Maitreya's words before, albeit in another guise. They will remember the Teacher Who appeared to them and planted the seeds of sharing and justice in their minds while endowing their lands with the Waters of Life from Aquarius.

Eventually so great will be the pressure for a better, a fairer and a safer world that even the most bigoted will add their voices to the clamour for change. Thus will it be.

15 July 2009
SI September 2009

The perennial light of Truth

One day in the winter of 1875, Helena Petrovna Blavatsky, one of the founders of the Theosophical Society, made a vow: to spread by every means in her power the teachings which she had received from several Masters of the Himalayan Lodge of the Spiritual Hierarchy of our planet. True to her vow, she set to work to inform the world of these teachings. Her books, *The Secret Doctrine*, *Isis Unveiled* and *The Key to Theosophy*, are testimony to her indefatigable industry and will, in the face of great physical illness. These seminal works have informed and inspired many thousands of true seekers over the years and continue to do so.

The general reception of these precious insights was altogether different: seldom have the work and gifts of a great initiate been so denigrated and ridiculed, especially by the religious and scientific communities of the day. Even now, after a hundred and thirty five or so years, Blavatsky is regularly dismissed as a charlatan, a spiritual medium and a "dishonest faker". So vehement and so worldwide was this condemnation that much of this negativity still clings to her name. And, to Theosophy itself.

Madame Blavatsky was 4.0 degrees initiate, almost a Master, equal in level to the Disciple Jesus and close to that of the great Leonardo da Vinci. How is it is possible that such a distinguished Toiler for the Good could be so maligned? Jesus himself is a prime example of how ignorance and fear can dominate the perceptions of men. Even while overshadowed by Maitreya the Christ, Jesus was made to suffer from these twin attributes of thoughtless men.

Today the world is grappling with many problems and, predictably, schisms have arisen in assessing these problems and in overcoming them. Men and women everywhere have different qualities of mind and brain, of openness or otherwise to ideas new and unfamiliar. They also stand at different points on a ladder of evolution and from near the bottom of the ladder the work and insights of many of those above them mean little or naught. Thus has it always been.

From now on, however, this age-old problem will be ameliorated to the benefit of all. The presence of Maitreya and a growing number of His group of Masters will bring to humanity a great leavening.

Much of the simpler levels of the Ageless Wisdom Teachings will be placed before the world as a whole, drawing more and more of the general public into Theosophy and its teachings. This will help to prepare large numbers to stand before the Initiator and to enter consciously into the Light.

In this way, many men and women, taking advantage of this new situation, will prosper greatly on their journey of evolution. When Maitreya steps forward, this process will begin. More and more, as they respond to Him, they will find growing within themselves an appetite for the truth, and a longing for wisdom and light.

5 September 2009
SI October 2009

Men's lives will flourish

When men more fully realize the extent of the damage done to their lives by the economic and financial collapse of recent years, they will find it impossible to revert, as many hope will be the case, to the old system. That economy was shattered by greed, selfishness and separation, but essentially by the action of the energies of the new time. Already, more than men are aware, the energies of Aquarius work their magic on Earth. Increasingly people are being drawn together in consciousness; the energies of synthesis are performing their beneficent work. Already, many are responding in a new way, as if relieved of a deadening weight, looking forward to a world simplified but more united.

When We see this, We too are gratified and strengthened in Our belief in the qualities of man. Our hope for the future is renewed as We see men search and respond to the new. The 'star' has not been alone in changing the atmosphere of Earth from despair to hope, but is proving a potent factor in this transformation. More and more the Aquarian energies will create in men the desire for unity and oneness, and even now are sowing the seeds of future transformation.

Maitreya, meanwhile, waits patiently for the day on which His face may be seen by men. That day is not far off. Already arrangements are being made for His initial interview, the first of many such. Do not be surprised if reactions to His statements are quiet or subdued. Have no doubt that in future appearances Maitreya will speak loudly and boldly for the suffering poor of the world, for an ending of war, for a world in which justice and sharing enfold men in their beneficent grace. Much, very much, is expected of Maitreya, but few can realize the vast extent of His generosity of spirit. People will come to know and love

Him as a friend and as a teacher, and will willingly respond to His words. Maitreya will evoke from men their own hearts' love for justice, sharing and peace, perennial jewels in the hearts of all men.

Now comes the time of a further flowering of these divine attributes as men reconsider the faults and inadequacies of the past. Under the guidance of Maitreya and His Group, men's lives will flourish as never before; raising men from their past state of ignorance and fear into the expression of a divinity until now almost unknown.

11 October 2009
SI November 2009

Men will answer the Call

Since the dawn of time, man has asked himself the question: why am I here, what is the meaning of life? Despite the teachings of the various religions and those of holy men of the past, most people are baffled and unsure whether there is, indeed, any purpose or meaning in what we call 'life', and wonder likewise what experience, if any, awaits us after 'death'.

In this coming time, the answers to these long-held worries and fears will become the common knowledge of all. This will in large measure be the result of the open presence of Maitreya and His Group of Masters. Your Elder Brothers will so stimulate the consciousness of men and so exemplify the teaching They give that in a relatively short period an enormous awakening will take place. Gone, for millions, will be the doubt and fear of the past. Men will know for sure, that they are, each one, engaged in a great adventure of discovery which will take them, in due course, to a perfection hitherto undreamed of. Such sense of meaning and purpose will replace the present arid and fearful doubt that an era of untold creativity and change will blossom and flourish. Thus will it be, and thus will men awaken to their destiny as exemplars of the divine. All men are divine but not all know this to be true. More and more, men will realize this truth and so change the world around them.

The Masters are readying Themselves for open recognition and work. Their presence will provide the confidence that the needed changes in our social life will be for the better and have long been necessary. The aim is that the Masters and men should work together in every field of endeavour, and thus expedite the changes required.

The first priority is that war must be abandoned for ever, utterly, totally. This requires a degree of trust as yet not known in the world. Sharing alone, it will be found, will manifest the needed trust and so create justice worldwide. Until justice reigns, there will never be true peace. Step by step, men will come to see this logic. They will come to understand that there is no alternative. If men would live and prosper they must abandon injustice and war. Can men meet the challenge? Men have faced and overcome many vicissitudes in their long sojourn on Earth. Today, led by Maitreya and His Group, they will be inspired to act for their own best interest and to answer the call for justice and sharing.

Many are the voices of the past which will call for caution and delay, but when men hear Maitreya's voice sound within their hearts, they will be kindled by a fiery longing for Justice and Peace, for Sharing and Right Relationship, for Brotherhood and Love.

Thus will it be.

8 November 2009
SI December 2009

A glorious enterprise

When humanity sees Maitreya, whether they recognize Him or not, they will feel obliged to support Him or to reject Him and all He stands for: sharing, justice and peace. Thus will men be divided and known. Thus will the Sword of Cleavage perform its destined task, and thus will Maitreya know the readiness of men for change. Appearing before men as one of them, the Great Lord ensures that men follow and support Him for the truth and sanity of His ideas rather than for His status.

Nevertheless, it matters not whether they recognize Him as Maitreya, as the Christ, or simply as a man Whose wisdom coincides with their own aspiration for justice and peace, for a better world for all men.

Gradually, we must assume, many will begin to see Maitreya as the One awaited by all religious groups under their various names, and will call Him thus. Some will say: "He must be the Mahdi," while others will declaim: "Krishna has come again, the law is fulfilled!" Others will ask: "Surely he is the Messiah, come at last," while still others will see Him as the Christ or Maitreya Buddha. All will see Him as their Expected One, fulfilling their hopes and come to fulfill their needs.

Maitreya will neither affirm nor deny these claims nor should those among His workers who believe they have recognized Him. Not until the Day of Declaration will Maitreya acknowledge His true identity and status.

On that glorious day men will know, beyond all gainsaying, that their long wait has not been in vain, that help, indeed, is at hand, that the Teacher is ready to aid and guide. That He comes as an Elder Brother rather than a Saviour, ready to take the lead to save our planet, and to enable men themselves to restore sanity to their lives and ways of living.

Maitreya will show that our problems are many but solvable. That the solution to all is already in our hands. That the simple act of sharing, alone, has the power to transform life on Earth for the better. He will ask for man's trust, as an Elder Brother, that He will not lead them into other than their destined path of harmony and love, that they have nothing to fear but their fear, and that the way ahead already has the blueprint of the Divine.

Thus will Maitreya ease the way for men to embark on a transformation huge in scope, involving all men and women everywhere, a transformation which will launch humanity into a glorious enterprise, the restoration of Planet Earth to its rightful place among its sister planets of our system.

10 January 2010
SI January/February 2010

The Awakening

Now that Maitreya has stepped forward into the open arena of the world and has appeared several times in full view of the television cameras, we can take stock of what has been achieved so far and, to some extent, interpret the reaction of those who have seen and heard Him. Bear in mind that in these preliminary approaches to the public, Maitreya has been careful not to frighten away those He wishes to help by too great an emphasis on change, too drastic and radical a programme for renewal. While critical of our present practices in financial matters, bringing pain and hardship to millions, He praised men for their many achievements and their readiness to aspire to the creation of a better world.

The response, so far, could be classified as muted but thoughtful, echoing the quiet earnestness of Maitreya's thought. One must remember that Maitreya was presented as an ordinary man, one of us, and not as a Messiah figure from on high. Thus, reactions of men were natural and honest, a true reflection of their fears and hopes. Of course, reactions varied with the background of the viewer, but Maitreya is well pleased with the response thus far.

From this point on, Maitreya will 'step up' the need for urgent change, the necessity for peace based on justice and sharing. He will also focus attention on the plight of planet Earth and the responsibility of men for its problems. Thus will the Great Lord orchestrate a mounting crescendo of action for the re-establishment of our world and life.

Interviews of this kind will continue to be given around the world, awakening men everywhere to their opportunity to set to rights their life, to create justice and peace by sharing, to see themselves as One, to end forever the competition and greed which for so long has held men back from their destined path to divinity.

Thus will Maitreya coax men out of their long slumber and awaken their desire for change. Thus will grow a great informed World Public Opinion, the greatest force on Earth.

Against that mighty force no reactionary platform can stand. Humanity itself, inspired and vitalized by Maitreya, will reinvent their future, and through freedom and justice for all establish the Era of Goodwill and Manifested Love.

9 February 2010
SI March 2010

Maitreya speaks

With every week that passes, the words and thoughts of Maitreya resonate in the minds of millions of people who know not the source of these inspiring ideas and hopeful concepts. Many ponder deeply on their meaning and vision and are strangely comforted. Others feel enabled and energized, filled with fresh courage and resolve. Still others wonder who this man can be, so simple and relaxed, yet wonderfully wise. Many are the feelings of delight and love that His appearances have wrought.

Of course, not all have found His ideas attractive, or if attractive, certainly utopian and unobtainable. Large numbers are cautious and slightly anxious, fearful that He may be the one they have been taught most to fear: simple and unassuming, wrapped in an aura of goodness and love.

Thus do the many types and levels of men make known their stance and readiness for change.

Meanwhile, the Masters prepare Their groups for the time immediately ahead. Men and women of every country are being brought together and trained for the tasks which await their skills and altruistic service. They know the needs of the new world and the priorities of action. Service is the key. When the call from Maitreya and men everywhere rings out, these valiant ones will arise in thousands to meet the challenge. Thus will begin a movement which, gathering momentum, will soon cover, and remake, the world.

The needs of every aspect, one by one, will be addressed: the feeding of millions, starving or near, through the production and distribution of food; the slow asphyxiation of humanity by deforestation; the overcoming of global warming; the ending of the "invisible peril"; the ending of the political/economic impasse; the resolution of left versus right political systems. Each of these enormous tasks requires solutions. Each is urgent but the priorities are that no one should go hungry in a world of plenty, and that our planet is sorely in need of succour.

Soon, the impact of Maitreya's ideas will begin to be seen. Already many, worldwide, respond to His influence, directly or otherwise. More and more, the impact of His thought will clarify the tangle of interests which today take 'centre stage' in public debate, and the needs of every man and family will emerge as the central core of humanity's problems.

Even now, in many countries, there is emerging a new sense of the need to rethink everything, root and branch, and the concepts of sharing, justice and fairness are growing apace. As the scope of Maitreya's appearances widens, these ideas can only be expected to flourish and grow.

Thus the conscience of men is awakening and moving in the direction of right relationship. Thus, simply and calmly, does the Great Lord work to purify and sanctify the affairs of men.

14 March 2010
SI April 2010

Men awaken to Maitreya

From now, men will take more seriously the idea that help is at hand, that they are not alone, not without aid in their grief and helplessness. Recent events have brought again to humanity the hope that, at the point of their greatest need, when they had all but relinquished hope of succour, somehow their prayers would be answered and their pain assuaged. So potent has been the response to the essence of Maitreya's words, however quietly or obliquely uttered, that many already feel heartened and reassured that all will be well, that the future for men will be just and kind, even better than they dared to hope. Many are already beginning to doubt that this man is really 'one of us', but is someone sent from above to answer their call for help, and to ease their burden. Many, doubtless, find His words unhelpful and obstructive to their desires, but many more, by far, sense the simple truth of His ideas, and await eagerly their fruition. Thus, quietly and steadily does Maitreya aid the plight of men. Some have already recognized Him and pray to Him. Others are glad to hear aloud the answers to their many problems and await the opportunity to play a part in their solution.

Thus do the simple words of Maitreya echo through the world. Thus do they awaken in men the hope of renewal. Where enough men are so awakened and ready for change Maitreya will increase the tempo and energy of His delivery and galvanize millions to call for action on their own behalf. Men must understand that action must come from themselves, else nothing new can happen. Where men realize this they will act, spontaneously and with hearts ablaze with hope. So will it be, and so will men fulfil their destiny and create the better framework for the new age which opens before them.

Maitreya is at the beginning only of His task to guide men into right relationship; but already He finds that His words encourage, and soon will galvanize, millions to act and claim their destiny, not through revolution but through revelation of their own divinity.

11 April 2010
SI May 2010

Brotherhood

Without doubt, this is a time of major importance to humanity. The decisions made by men now will decide, in large measure, the whole future of this planet. Future generations will marvel at the apparent ease with which so many today slough off concern for the world's ills: millions starve and die of want in a world blessed with a huge surplus of food; millions more are always hungry and undernourished. Many know this to be true yet do nothing. How can this be? What prevents their action? The basis of this inaction is complacency, the source of all evil in the world. Complacency has its roots in the crime of separation which pulls men apart and prevents the flowering of Brotherhood.

Men soon must realize this truth or perish. Brotherhood is both an idea and the fact of our planetary life. Without the reality of Brotherhood as the basis for all action, man's every effort would come to nothing.

When men accept Brotherhood as the essential nature of life, every aspect of our daily living will change for the better. Every manifestation of Brotherhood melts the barriers which form themselves between men, and lead to misunderstanding and distrust. Brotherhood assuages the pain of loss and misfortune. It is a precious gift to be cultivated and nourished. Treasure Brotherhood, it is the key which gives entry to the finest chambers of the heart. We, your Elder Brothers, cherish Brotherhood as Our highest nature, and strive to maintain and strengthen its reality. When men, too, grasp the beneficent truth of Brotherhood, they will realize the beauty which its nature displays, and grasp something of the beauty of divinity itself. Brotherhood is divine as men are divine. It could not be otherwise.

Men are about to experience a profound truth, an awareness of their essential Being. For most, it will come as an experience of rebirth to a state long lost in the distant past. Each, in his own way, will feel redeemed, made new, cleansed and purified. The joy and beauty of Brotherhood will thrill through their Being, and each will see themselves as a part of that beauty and love.

12 May 2010
SI June 2010

The search for peace

Without doubt, the most important achievement by humanity would be the ending of war. This achieved, men's energies would be released to tackle the many other pressing problems which beset them today: the millions who starve needlessly in a world of plenty; the precarious ecological imbalance of the planet; the ever-widening gap between the developed rich and the developing poor nations; the growing incidence and fear of terrorism, ever more sophisticated; the hardship and fear engendered by the economic collapse around the world.

Some governments try to cope with some of these difficult problems while still others are main culprits and instigators of them. What can humanity do? How to start when each problem grows out of another, and all seem intractable?

From Our viewpoint, these problems are real and pressing, and stem from one single condition: the separatism which sits like a heavy yoke on the shoulders of humanity and prevents all action in unison. Ideology rather than reason still guides the minds and actions of governments whose decisions affect the lives of all. They seek friends and allies to support their position, and thus are built the power blocks which strive for supremacy in the minds and hearts of men.

Today, this problem is increased by the re-opening of the religious divide between Christianity and Islam. In a growingly secular world, the fundamentalist adherents of both religions are more and more bellicose, raising the temperature of confrontation to ever more dangerous heights. In particular, Islamic terrorism, in complete contradiction to the teaching of the Prophet, has brought a new dimension to the struggle for a peaceful world. How can this process be reversed? There is but one way to grapple with these problems, one which has never been tried but which, at a stroke, would ease the lot of countless millions and bring, at long, long last, true and lasting peace to a world in agony.

Men must realize that they are not separate, never were and never shall be, that they are part of a divine and seamless whole which enfolds us all, to which, in our own way, we give the name of God. Men must realize that God is peace, is justice, sharing and trust, and that their fear is also the fear of their brothers. Maitreya's task is to show men this truth, and to remind them that at the core of their yearning lies the peace they all desire, waiting to be made manifest.

13 June 2010

SI July/August 2010

A new light in humanity

Already, the Forces of Light are gaining ground, making progress, winning hearts and minds. Even now, it is possible to predict a sure and safe outcome to the struggle which has been raging, albeit unknown to the majority of men, for the future of planet Earth and its inhabitants.

For countless ages, that struggle has been fought on every plane, in all conditions and situations, and is the very fabric of the history of the world. At long, long last, a new light can be observed in the aura of the race of men, one that augurs well for the future of the race. From where does this new light come? It is, of course, the result of many happenings and benedictions, but above all, it is the sign that men are beginning to see themselves in a new light, beginning to sense themselves as at least potentially divine, certainly more worthy and meaningful than they had thought, and capable of creating a world in which they can take pride.

Notwithstanding the pain and suffering so widespread today, many are sensing a new confidence in themselves and in the future, a new hope that the present ills are transitory, and that a better time is near.

Seeing this new light within humanity, Maitreya knows that men are awakening to His efforts and energies, that the new potencies of Aquarius are fulfilling their promise, and are drawing men together in a sensed unity of purpose and pride.

From now on, this dawning sense of unity, and the strength which it engenders, will manifest itself more and more, and will lead to organized action by many to better their lot, to change conditions which belittle men and leave them helpless. In this way, a substantial change in world conditions will take place in a relatively short period of time. Men are approaching the nadir of their self-induced misfortune.

Destructiveness and war, complacency, selfishness and greed, have all played a part in creating these painful conditions. The awakening, the new light, is a sign that men are beginning to understand the Great Law: harmlessness, alone, brings men into correct relation with the Law of Cause and Effect, the fundamental Law of our lives. This is a spiritual truism but one that the race of men has found difficult to understand or accept. Such an understanding and acceptance would change for ever, and at a stroke, much unnecessary pain and suffering in our world.

The Aquarian Energies, gathering potency with every day that passes, will make it easier for men to see the need for harmlessness. These benign forces work towards fusion and synthesis and so lessen the desire for competition and assertive individualism. The signs are beginning to show that man is on his way.

11 July 2010
SI September 2010

Earth transformed

In some twenty years from now, any visitor to Earth would be amazed by the transformation that he would find in every aspect of our lives. The best of the past will have been preserved but a new and vigorous beauty will prevail everywhere, and a new relationship will have been established between people and the environment in which they live. Gone for ever will be the slums and hovels in which millions today eke out a 'living'. A new pride in 'Man' will generate an equal concern for men's leisure and social activities, and lead gradually to a new understanding of man's essential needs. New technology will free countless millions from the drudgery of repetitive work; the demand for knowledge in every field will open wide the doors of colleges, factories and farms alike, and a new enthusiasm for learning will manifest throughout the world. Thus will men understand better the underlying purposes of our incarnational experiences and so will grow the needed control of our physical, astral and mental equipment. This will lead men to the door of Initiation and thus to perfectionment.

Thus will men return anew to the age-old Path to Perfection and, freed from the glamours and errors of the past, tread once more the way of sacrifice, of renunciation of all that hinders the highest understanding and light. Man has strayed far from this simple path, sidetracked by a gross materialism which has lured him to the very edge of disaster. But, as men will find, their eternal divinity has, once more, asserted itself and drawn man back from the brink.

A growing number of people, everywhere, are beginning to sense this to be true, and to awaken to the task of transformation. In this way, they find their own sense of responsibility enhanced, and respond accordingly. Thus are the workers of the future found and thus too does the world change for the better.

Quietly as yet, but steadily, does Maitreya work to potentize this process. His beneficent energies act like yeast to raise the aspiration and strengthen the resolve of all who can respond. These are many, and so is built a great army of workers in the light, the light that will transform the world and ensure the future for all men.

13 September 2010
SI October 2010

Man's ultimate triumph

The future life for humanity will prove to be not only more just and less stressful, but infinitely more interesting than it is now for many millions of people. The work of reconstruction is so vast that, in that area alone, the creative powers of many will find endless stimulus. Later, as the preliminary teaching of a more esoteric nature is deemed desirable, the flood-gates will open wide and an extraordinary pent-up thirst for knowledge will manifest around the world. Men will be astonished by what there is to know, and will eagerly act to quench their thirst. An enormous educational programme will provide the required knowledge and understanding. The reality of Initiation as a prime factor in the evolutionary journey will inspire thousands to take in hand their own evolution, and so to undertake the necessary refinement of their vehicles. With some Masters working openly, an extraordinary stimulus will be given to this work and much will be accomplished in a relatively very short time. Nearly five million people already stand at the threshold of the first Initiation. Their number will be increased by many thousands before long.

Thus will the Mysteries of the Initiatory process inspire and galvanize humanity to place its steps solidly on the Path to Liberation.

Such a view, at this time, might seem far from the reality, even somewhat naïve, but the outward presence of Maitreya and His group of Masters will have an amazing impact on the minds and hearts of literally millions of people in every country. These will now stand ready, their aspiration high and pure, for the creation of a new world, and for an entirely new view of what it means to be alive on planet Earth. Many of them, perhaps the majority, are young and relatively untarnished by the cynicism and unfettered greed of their elders. Thus they see clearly the answers to the problems which confound their fathers, blinded as they are by the faults and glamours of the past. These young people will remake this world for their fathers. They have come into incarnation for this purpose and will answer Maitreya's Call. They come, too, many of them, trained and prepared for the tasks which await them and which, undaunted, they will gladly perform.

Have no fear, the world is safe in these young hands. They await, eagerly, the opportunity to serve and save. Many, today see clearly the faults and weaknesses of men; few, indeed, can see the Divinity which gives Us, your Elder Brothers, the sure knowledge of man's ultimate triumph.

11 October 2010
SI November 2010

The needs of men

When men take stock of their present situation they can come to but one conclusion: the methods of even the recent past no longer work. On all sides, but particularly in the financial and economic sector, there is continuous and growing chaos. 'Experts' are summoned to aid the floundering governments regain some control but to no avail; the old, tried methods refuse to obey the wills of their chancellors, however experienced they might be.

What are they, the governments of the world, to do? What *can* they do? They can continue for a time manipulating the old structures, hoping that things will 'settle down', and the old patterns survive. This is, indeed, a forlorn hope. Generally speaking, the governments of most countries see their role as protectors and upholders of the 'status quo', that false idea that life is static and, therefore, all change is rebellion and undesirable.

This attitude is true of most governments, whether of the 'right' or the 'left', capitalistic or socialistic. In either case they fail to recognize the yearnings of their peoples for change, for a new concept of living, one that ensures their ability to raise their families in peace, security and well-being. The failure of governments is precisely their failure to see that their true role is to look after the well-being of their people. Lost as they are in competition and the following of 'market forces', they have lost touch, for the most part, with the needs of those whom they claim to represent. The glamours of power and authority overcome, as often as not, their desire to serve.

Divorced from the real needs of the people, they fall back on ideology and theory. Even so, they are not entirely to be blamed. They know nothing of the forces with which they try to contend. Ignorant as they are, they fall easy prey to the destructive forces of the past.

The people, meanwhile, suffer and wait and pray, unaware, for the most part, that the help for which they pray is even now among them, ready and eager to aid their suffering and to ease their lot. The people know the true nature of their need but require a strong and fearless representative to give it voice. Already present, that representative, Maitreya, is working quietly to influence the direction which events will take. Soon, that voice will strike a stronger note, and many will be ready to respond. Thus the Plan works out its beneficent purpose to secure the future for all men.

13 November 2010
SI December 2010

Man's essential Brotherhood

For untold ages, man has wandered the Earth for sustenance, gain, security and peace. As tribes and even nations, he has criss-crossed the planet over and over again, fighting with, and intermarrying with, a long succession of disparate peoples. The result of this endless wandering is the One humanity today. No matter the differences in colour, religion, tradition and language, all men are descendents of common ancestors and have evolved by the same means to their present state. That this present state undoubtedly favours some groups over others is the result of many historical factors, and not of any innate difference in intelligence or adaptability. Throughout history, groups have risen to prominence for a longer or shorter time, only to sink back into obscurity again, leaving their creativity to remind later generations of their presence.

All of this being true, it is essential for modern humanity to see itself as One, and the differences in appearance the result of relatively recent climatic conditions, together with the different ray influences which have manifested regularly through the emerging racial types. Humanity is still evolving in consciousness, together, as One.

Advancing together, each race and sub-race adds some new quality to the whole. The process of repeated incarnations ensures that gradually, each individual inherits the new knowledge and awareness of the epoch. If men truly understood the complexity and beauty of this process, gone for ever would be the dislike and distrust, the 'racism' of today. Men would realize that, in truth, they are brothers; journeying together on a seemingly endless voyage of self-discovery.

When We, your Elder Brothers, work more openly, you will find that this truth is central in Our understanding of man's nature and relationship. The human family is the nourishing base of our lives. In it we learn to co-operate and thus create together, fashioning the rich tapestry of our shared identity.

How, then, can men come to this essential understanding? We, the Brotherhood, will demonstrate this relationship in all We do, and men will come to see themselves thus, as brothers all. Sharing will bring men to this happy pass and will glorify them in their new demonstration of truth. So shall it be.

Then will men conquer the heights of achievement, sharing their knowledge and experience. Gone for ever will be the false barriers which men have erected to keep at a distance their brothers, realizing them at last as themselves.

17 January 2011
SI January/February 2011

The voice of the people is heard

During eighteen momentous days, recently, the attention of the world was fixed on one square in one ancient city. In their thousands and tens of thousands, the people of Cairo, young and old and very young, walked bravely past the tanks and water canons, and learned quickly the art of breathing amid tear-gas assault. The people of Cairo, in peaceful brotherhood, took over and held their Square, adding the name Tahrir to the glories of Egypt's illustrious past.

For eighteen days they defied the police and agents of the old, corrupt regime, calling with one peaceful and confident voice for change, for justice and jobs, for freedom and the rule of law. The Muslims among them prayed at the appointed times while others stood guard, protecting them from attack. Brotherhood blossomed and an extraordinary spiritual potency was tangible in the Square and throughout the city.

From whence did this come? Every day, for eighteen days, Maitreya spent many hours in Cairo, mainly in the Square. In many different guises, He worked among the people, consoling the wounded and the many martyrs who gave their lives for freedom and justice. The Great Lord encouraged, guided and blessed them for their ardour and restraint, and a deep sense of love and unity filled the hearts and minds of all the people. Foreign journalists were astonished by the joy expressed so openly by the citizens, young and old, rich and poor, lame and hearty. Bathing in the energies and love of Maitreya, they were born anew.

Nearby despots and 'strong men' watched these daily scenes on television in horror and disbelief, expecting a sure and firm response from the old regime to end this madness. This madness was the voice of the new time, the time of justice and sharing, freedom and love.

It is the voice of the people, and the people have awakened to their unity and power. For the old despots, the writing is on the wall.

13 February 2011
SI March 2011

Man's responsibility

From the earliest times, mankind has feared the natural disturbances of our planetary home. Cataclysms of unimaginable ferocity have destroyed huge areas of the Earth's surface over and over again. This fact is hard for many to accept and raises, always, grave doubts in the minds of many religious people about the veracity of God's love for humanity. How can we believe in a loving God who allows thousands of people to be killed in earthquakes, tsunamis and the rest? Were humanity to understand their own involvement in such planetary destruction, they could play a significant role in preventing its occurrence.

The Earth's crust, as it has evolved over the ages, is not single and evenly spread around the world. As is well known, it takes the form of various plates at different depths, which overlap and are in relatively constant movement. Countries and cities which lie on or near the plate edge, or fault-lines, are consequently subjected to earthquakes and, if near oceanic regions, tsunamis. It is not a question of God's love failing humanity but of seismic pressure which must be released. What, we may ask, causes seismic pressure to grow to such a destructive extent?

Elemental Devas (or Angelic forces) oversee the mechanism by which these colossal energies act or are modified. The Earth is a living Entity and responds to the impact of these forces in various ways. One major source of impact comes directly from humanity. As humanity, in its usual competitive way, creates tension through wars, and political and economic crisis – that is when we are out of equilibrium – so too do the Devic lives go out of equilibrium. The inevitable result is earthquakes, volcanic eruptions and tsunamis. We are responsible.

How then to end this cycle of destruction? Humanity has the means but so far lacks the will to change. We must see ourselves as One, each man and woman a reflection of the Divine, brothers and sisters, sons and daughters of the One Father. We must banish war for ever from this Earth; we must share the resources of this planet which belong to all. We must learn to live in harmony with the planet itself to know a future of harmony with each other.

Maitreya has come to show men the way, and to galvanize man's actions. Across the globe, men are finding their voice and calling for justice and freedom. Many have died to claim their right, God given, to freedom and justice. His call is for all men and women everywhere to see themselves as He sees them, as Divine, Sons and Daughters of Divinity Itself.

13 March 2011
SI April 2011

The ways of the New Time

Recent events in the Middle East have brought humanity face to face with a number of problems. The Western powers have become embroiled, largely against their will, in a Libyan civil war which they did not recognize as such. Their main concern was to safeguard an uninterrupted flow of oil, close at hand, in Libya. They also wanted to help the people of Benghazi facing slaughter by the forces of an ageing, quixotic tyrant, who had watched aghast at the apparently successful overthrow by its people of a powerful neighbouring tyranny.

Little did the Western powers know that the peaceful protests of the Egyptian people had escalated in Libya into armed revolution without the planning, leadership or arms to ensure success.

The United Nations agreed a mandate for a no-fly-zone but should have followed it up with a UN peacekeeping force, hopefully drawn from the Arab countries. Failure to do so has precipitated the present difficult situation for all concerned.

Under the impact of the powerful energies now focused by Maitreya and His group, the people of the Middle East are undergoing a great awakening, and are demanding new freedoms and participation in the management of their lives. Nor are these demands confined to the Middle East. More and more, these same demands for participation and justice are being heard throughout the world. The young in particular are sensing the need for a new kind of world, one which allows them to develop and express themselves, free from the old dogmas of their elders. What we are witnessing is nothing less than a renaissance of the young people of the Earth, freeing themselves from the tyranny of hatred and war, bigotry and separation. Nothing can for long halt their progress. This is the New Time and the young are testing themselves in the struggle for new life.

The old order is deeply entrenched and hard to overcome. The old tyrants in every field of life are loath to forgo their power and wealth, and fight hard against the tide of change, but they fight against the energies and will of Divinity Itself, and must give way in due course. A greater power than that of all the powerful on this Earth demands expression and nothing can prevent its manifestation. It is the way of the future, planned from the beginning of the world.

Nothing can halt its progress and the young are its harbingers. Listen keenly to the young, they have the future safely in their hearts. Not for nothing was it the young of Tahrir Square who sat at Maitreya's feet as He taught them the ways of the future, the ways of the New Time, the Time of Peace, Justice and Sharing, of Freedom and Love.

11 April 2011
SI May 2011

The way of the future

In a very few years time, the present period of stress and hardship will be much allayed. Behind the scenes, much is changing. Many of the forces which have brought about the conflict and struggle of today are weakening, and are being replaced by forces altogether more favourable to men. So many different energies, and direction of these energies, are simultaneously involved at the present moment that it is difficult to ascertain precisely when this change will begin, but it should not be much more than about two years before the first clear signs of change are discernable. There will follow a period of change which few would conceive possible in so short a period of time: the present upsurge of demands for freedom and involvement in their own destiny which has been manifested so strongly by the people of the Middle East will sweep across the world and involve country after country, large and small. Thus will the Voice of the People grow ever stronger and more eloquent. More and more, men and women everywhere will begin to understand clearly their needs and their invincible strength to claim their birthright.

Inevitably, some countries will find the changes easier to achieve than will others. Some will find that the groups who, for centuries, have wielded power and built their citadels of wealth will be loath to relinquish that supremacy, but the forces for change will become so insistent and unstoppable that they, too, will have to alter their direction and adjust to the demands of their people.

Thus a new society will evolve with remarkable speed, one that holds sacred the right of all people to self-determination, the democratic right to involvement in their society and their future; their right to adequate living standards, healthcare and education. Above all, men will claim the right to live in peace.

Maitreya will sustain men in their demands for justice and freedom and will magnetise their every effort. As He did in Cairo, He will be with all who make their demands in peace, respecting all groups and all religions, without rancour and competition. Thus will men come to understand the way of the future, the only way which will guarantee that future, a future shared by all, without division.

8 May 2011
SI June 2011

The path to Unity

When the history of this unique time is written, men will realize, perhaps for the first time, how important, how central, have been the recent events in the Middle East. In an astonishing six months, following the example of the people of Tunisia and Egypt, the inhabitants of many Middle Eastern countries, subdued, and locked into centuries-old tribal dictatorial regimes, have risen and demanded their right to freedom and democracy, to social justice and work. What media call 'the Arab Spring' is costing many lives and much suffering for these courageous people who die willingly for freedom for their brothers and children. They are called, and are indeed, martyrs.

From now on, this same phenomenon will manifest throughout the world. Already, many peoples are organizing themselves to do likewise. A blueprint for change has caught the imagination of many millions and soon will command the attention of the world. Men have understood that, when organized and brave, they are invincible. Nothing can halt this movement for change. It embodies the concepts of the future and of the Plan. Maitreya has given it voice, which is now the voice of the peoples of the world.

The old order seeks in every way to halt the progress of this movement for change, but it cannot stand for ever against the principles of life: ever changing, ever remaking its form to better express the nature of that life. Thus is it today, and thus the old will wither and the new shoots flourish, as men seek to express and manifest better the principles of the New Time: sharing, justice, right relationship, love and unity.

Man, verily, is on his way. Naught can halt his further progress if he thinks in terms of Unity. All men seek Unity but are confused by different paths. Hold ever before you the principles of Unity and Love, and the way discloses itself.

Thus spoke Maitreya in Cairo, in Tahrir Square. The best of those who heard Him will lead their brothers and sisters and show them the way, the simple way to Brotherhood and Peace, Justice and manifested Love.

11 June 2011
SI July/August 2011

Change towards Unity

When men eventually take stock of their present situation they must surely admit that all is not well for humanity. Political, economic, social, environmental conditions are filled with problems which test the resources of all the countries to the limit. Even those countries which seem to be economically dominant at the present time have problems which deny them the ease their wealth implies. What is preventing the nations from achieving a degree of balance and well-being? Why do even old, rich and experienced nations plunge suddenly into chaos and strife? Why the pain and struggle for so many; what prevents a greater sense, and expression, of unity?

The answers to these questions are many and varied, but the single inclusive factor is the time, the moment in this Earth's history, in which they are being asked.

This time is like none other in the history of the world. The changes taking place are momentous, beyond human comprehension, and will alter life, as we now know it, profoundly and for ever.

On every plane these changes are taking place, some slowly, even in the very fabric of the Earth's crust; others in a growing momentum which challenges men's capacity for correct response.

Useless, in this context, are the tired ideas of backward-looking politicians, steeped in the glamours of position and power. Today, it is the people who are ahead of their leaders, and are voicing aloud their understanding and needs. In country after country, the voice of the people is becoming more focused and distinct. Millions are now educated and sure of their needs: peace, work and hope for their future. A growing sense of unity, too, is beginning to inform their expectations and demands. They know they are not alone in the world but have millions of brothers and sisters everywhere, with the same problems and needs.

In this way, even if unaware of His presence and teachings, they are responding to Maitreya's energy and influence, and building the framework of the future.

14 August 2011
SI September 2011

Creating the Sword of Cleavage

From time to time, there appears among men a figure who embodies the best, or the worst, that men can show. These individuals become the most loved or the most hated of men. In either case, they usually draw to themselves many followers or devotees. Such figures have enormous magnetic appeal for the majority of men or, on occasion, are an inspiring example of destructive power on a large scale. The history books are full of examples of both types.

Today, in large numbers, many examples of both types are manifesting worldwide. The effect of this manifestation is to set before humanity two opposing lines of action, and so create the tension of choice which will determine the future of the race. In biblical terms this is the 'Sword of Cleavage'. For many years the energies emanating from, and directed by Maitreya have sought to create such confrontation of opposites. This may seem strange indeed to many people but it is essential that humanity make the correct choices for its future. Otherwise that future would be bleak indeed.

The Sword of Cleavage is the energy we call Love: wielded by Maitreya it sets "brother against brother" and tests the true divine consciousness of men everywhere. The ultimate aim of all evolution is to establish on Earth the 'Kingdom of God', and the Sword of Cleavage shows men the way.

The teaching of Maitreya is simple. One might think that His priorities would seem obvious to all men; sadly this is not the case. Maitreya presents a future of tranquillity and peaceful endeavour as the inevitable result of sharing and justice for all, the creation of a world "where no man lacks, where no two days are alike, where the Joy of Brotherhood manifests through all men". How is it possible, you might think, to gainsay such a message of hope? Is this not the future yearned for by everyone? It is the future hoped for by the majority of men, but not by all. Humanity stands on different rungs of the evolutionary ladder; above a certain level all bodes well for men. It is those who have not as yet manifested that measure of their divine Self who do not recognize that sharing is divine, that justice and right relationship are divine, but who see Divinity as competition and conflict, and register a man's worth by the weight of his gold.

Many are fearful and suffering; bereft of work and hope for the future, they struggle from day to day. But many others are making their future for themselves, and many, too, are dying in the process. Throughout the world men are awakening to the possibility of a better life with freedom and justice at its heart. Have no fear, the people's voice is rising and like a contagion affecting more and more. Maitreya stands behind those who live – or die – for the truth of freedom, justice and the unity of man. The young lead the way, and the future is for them.

8 September 2011
SI October 2011

Maitreya's promise

While many people continue to believe that the present banking and stock exchange systems are necessary and unalterable, more and more are coming to the conclusion that they have passed their usefulness and must soon be replaced. Too many are suffering from the effects of unfettered greed, and yearn for greater justice and fairness in order to survive what is so glibly called 'the current economic climate'. Before the economic collapse of 2008, at least in the developed world, there was plenty of money. People had work and houses to live in; new millionaires were born everyday. Elsewhere, of course, millions still starved and millions more went hungry, but for some there was plenty of money and life felt good.

Where has all the money gone? What has happened to it? Now, no one has work and the money has disappeared – into the banks and disappeared. And the millionaires are now billionaires. It is all very puzzling. A conjuring, a confidence trick, you would think, has been played on half the world.

Will the old ways, the old time, return? Do we really want them to return with the wealth of the rich doubling daily and the poor picking up the coppers they let fall?

The people everywhere are sensing a change and are lending their voices to its call. They are sensing, too, their power to act, and many die to prove it. They sense that the old ways are almost over and have spent their force. They feel that there are other, better ways to live and look forward to tomorrow. Verily, the old ways are dying and hold back the race. The wheel turns and mighty Rome is falling once again. Maitreya's fire is lit in the hearts of countless millions and they respond, eager to build a new world where justice and harmony rule. Maitreya's promise is that this new world is on its way.

9 October 2011
SI November 2011

The Herald of the New

Many will remember the present time as a time of trial, of tension and upheaval. Actually, seen with the more discerning eye, it is a time of renewal, of preparation for a new beginning. Thus may men take great hope from the present changes. The past has had its day and is fast failing to benefit the race. The young grow weary and fretful from its long dominion, and turn to drugs and crime to ease their souls' ennui and despair.

Meantime, the Herald of the New is quietly inspiring a new generation of activists who will emerge in every nation, mindful of the needs of men everywhere. Already, as you know, the groups of activists for the new structures are working openly and courageously in many lands, showing a new aspiration which is forming in the hearts of millions: respect for, and co-operation with, all, and an end to the old divisive greed.

Thus are men finding the blueprint of the future time, by renewing themselves in the simple teaching of Maitreya. Peace and Justice are beginning to take centre stage in the minds of millions. When men realize that sharing alone will bring these cherished concepts into being they will embark on a transformation of society beyond anything envisaged until now. Stage by stage, these changes will be adopted and tried out for general use. The pain and sense of loss of today will give way to renewed hope and satisfaction that the world is at last on the right path and thus experiments can be safely undertaken.

Thus will disappear the fear of change. Great transformations will proceed in ordered sequence as men realize the beauty of the new forms. Gradually, the old, divisive ways of the past will be seen as the mistakes of the past and die out, useless to the new unity.

The words and example of Maitreya will hasten the sense of the unity, which will more and more manifest the energies of Aquarius, drawing men into a synthesis unknown today.

At the present time, the Masters in Their various centres work through Their groups to bring about these changes with the minimum of social upheaval. Theirs is the task to empower change at an acceptable rate with evolution rather than revolution. This is not easy to do, for men, when young, are impatient for the new, and when old, are resistant to change. Thus the present turmoil.

Many await this time with hope and joy. Many more are locked in hopelessness and fear. Many are eager to see the future world free from war and destitution. Many more wait wearily for their burden to lighten.

Maitreya will awaken men to their destiny and free them from fear and doubt. He will free them, too, from the constant sense of alienation and distrust. Men's long winter in the wilderness has prepared them for the simpler, happier times ahead.

12 November 2011
SI December 2011

The Great Decision

Steadily, humanity moves forward to its Great Decision. Unbeknown to all but a few, men are being tested as never before in their long history on Earth.

The Sword of Cleavage, wielded by Maitreya, the Christ and World Teacher, is doing its beneficent work: separating and dividing men, accentuating their different natures and proclivities.

In this way, the choice before men becomes clearer, more sharply defined. Maitreya's energy of love is impersonal, it stimulates everyone, those who long for peace and right relations, and those who love greed and competition, risking thereby a final war and total self-destruction. Thus the importance of the choice faced now by all.

Many might wonder that such a choice is necessary. Surely no-one wants a devastating war? Today, a small and local war could become a major war of nuclear dimension. The result would be too terrible to contemplate, yet there are those who, even now, are planning how to survive such an eventuality.

The choice for men is clear: to continue recklessly on the present greedy course and destroy life on planet Earth for ever, or to follow the promptings of the benevolent heart and practise sharing and justice as the only guarantee of a peaceful future for men of Earth.

The events of the Arab Spring are a sign that the young are responding to Maitreya's Call. Ahead of their elders, they have awakened to the new energies of Aquarius and the promise of the new life that they bring. They have lost all fear and gladly sacrifice themselves for a new-found freedom and dignity. A new splendour is growing among the young.

Throughout the world, groups plot and plan for revolution. Arms in many countries are now stockpiled for this purpose. Not revolution but evolution is Maitreya's advocacy. He knows well that revolution precipitates conflict and carnage, replacing one set of problems by another. What is required is a step by step process of change which allows everyone the experience of being involved in their own destiny.

Sharing is the sole means of ensuring such a process; sharing alone will engender the trust essential even to begin. Maitreya has said: "The first step into sharing is the first step into your Divinity." Accept sharing therefore, and enter into your birthright.

15 Janaury 2012
SI January/February 2012

The coming transformation

From the depth of its present problems and sorrows, humanity will find hope. So much that is taking place is positive and auspicious for the race that men can be assured of an early lessening of their problems, not all at once, but gradually, little by little. Gradually, also, men will learn the true reasons for their present anguish. They will come to understand that humanity is One, integral and related by long association and common ancestry, related, too, by its common divinity. No more need man fear and fight his neighbour, no longer need millions starve amidst plenty. Thus can be born a new time, a time when Justice and Sharing control the present chaos and irresponsibility, a time when men respect and care for one another, when the divinity of men becomes manifest and the secrets of life known. Sufficiency will replace abundance as the aim of sane men.

Thus will men come into right relationship with each other and with the Source of all. Under the inspiration and guidance of Maitreya and His group men will blossom in their divinity and make that manifest in all they do. The abominations of war and terror will fast fade from their memory, and a vast creative burgeoning will take their place.

Men will renew and beautify their cities, making them worthy of the new time. These will be greater in number and smaller in size, linked by transport, fast and noiseless. People will educate their children in many different ways, each child linked to the educational system as determined by their rays. In time the interchange between the Masters and the race of men will grow in ever increasing closeness, and children will move happily and logically from stage to stage in growing awareness. In all these measures, in this transformation, each one will play his part.

Presently, there will appear a series of signs which will mystify those who experience them. No one will be able to explain this phenomenon but it will presage a change in the thinking and understanding of men. From that time onwards, a sense of expectancy will grip most nations, which will prepare men for the extraordinary events that are to come. As you know, not all men take seriously the new time which lies ahead for mankind. These happenings will prepare more for this revelation.

12 February 2012
SI March 2012

Youth at the helm

This year, 2012, is one of great importance. It is essential that the impetus of the Arab Dawn, and its repercussions worldwide, be not lost. The Voice of the People, so vigorous and confident now, must continue to ring out through all the world, affirming Sharing and Justice as the only way to engender trust and a safer world for all. The remedy for men's ills is so simple, so easy of achievement, yet so difficult for many to grasp. Men must realise that every other method has been tried and has failed, ending inevitably in war.

Today, let all be assured, another major war would be nuclear, and would destroy, utterly, all life on Earth. Today, also, there are forces who are already planning how best to survive such annihilation, all to no avail. What can, and should, humanity do?

Broadly speaking, the governments today are organisations of elderly men who know no other way to work and govern than the ways of their youth, the ways of the past. They have little sense of why their methods no longer work. They know nothing of the new energies and impulses which flood the world today, and are baffled and betrayed by their inability to control events.

To a large extent, today, the People's Voice is the voice of the young. Governments, and the media under their control, largely ignore or vilify the voices and aspirations of the young; yet it is the young who have the answers, who understand that humanity is One, who call for fairness, for justice and sharing, and an end to war. The voice of such young people can never be silenced, and will not for long be ignored. The Voice of the People, young and old, will drown the whimpers of the men of money and lead humanity to the New Dawn. So will it be.

1 March 2012
SI April 2012

Water into wine

As is so often the case, Europeans are searching for an ever elusive unity. This time the problem is mainly economic. The Common Market, in this testing economic crisis, is fraying at the seams and losing its precarious unity.

The USA, in election year, treads carefully, anxious to see an upturn in trade and a down-turn in responsibility abroad. Israel, therefore is emboldened to take over the task of pressuring Iran. Meanwhile, China is booming and waxing rich while neighbouring Russia apes the USA of the 1930s. Thus the diehards of the old order struggle to keep the leaking ship afloat in the maelstrom of the new and more just energies of Aquarius. The Age of Synthesis is upon us, recognised or not, and every new day etches its stamp on the world.

Only the young, and the young in heart, it would seem, recognise the dimensions of this change. They alone know that justice and love can never be cast aside without pain. So it is with the young today who recognise a new note in Earth's song and seek, by all means open to them, to make it heard. Vast numbers throughout the world are beginning to respond to this new theme and search for valid means to implement their longing for change.

Many are beginning to grasp the essentials of life and with courage bear witness to their truth: Sharing, Justice and Love, they comprehend, are the essential ingredients of a civilisation based on the understanding that all men are Gods. In this way the world is slowly being prepared for an entirely new conception of the meaning of life.

Tirelessly, Maitreya and His group teach the age old way to happiness and divinity, for these two are one. When men truly understand this simple law they will gladly renounce the patterns of the past: the unholy divide which sustains the greed of so many, the disdain of the rich for the poor and the lust for power and war.

They will put behind them this dross which has gripped their imagination for so long. They will listen keenly to the Masters' advice and will, themselves, change water into wine.

15 April 2012
SI May 2012

The path of co-operation

When men realise the benefits of co-operation they will adopt it naturally as the most pleasant and intelligent way to proceed. Gone for ever will be the hardship and tension of constant competition, the strain of which saps the joy of work and makes each day a struggle for existence. Of course, there are many who adore this competitive struggle, who find in competition the stimulus that for them makes life worth living, pitting their frail egos against the rest. They need competition to register themselves to themselves. However, in the time immediately ahead, men, more and more responding to the beneficent energies of Aquarius, will realise the divisive nature of competition and will gladly acquire the habit of co-operation. In this way the world will reap an enormous benefit, as men work together as equals in the many tasks of reconstruction which will await their service. Thus will the world be transformed by willing hands. Thus will the new world be wrought.

Aquarius is another word for unity, and through its gift of co-operation that unity will gradually become manifest. Unity will be the hallmark of the new time.

For countless thousands of years, competition has held sway. Many are the achievements by which the habit of competition has enriched the forward striving of the race, but significant as these may be, they are as naught against the possibilities which co-operation would have allowed. As civilisations have marked the progress of man, the highest inspirations have sprung from co-operative effort, and have beckoned men forward. Today humanity has come to a turning point. Man's ever-enquiring mind and competitive spirit have brought the race to its most dangerous point in history. The desire for ultimate power in its most material form has given us the atomic bomb and a life of misery for millions. Man has thus to enter gladly a new path that will bring an end to destructive rivalry and war, or face oblivion itself. This is the choice which now faces the race of men. Each one must think deeply and take his stand.

9 May 2012
SI June 2012

The forerunners

Among humanity today is a growing number of men and women who are engaged in outlining the principles on which the new civilisation will be built. They are to be found in almost every country, and they propagate the teachings which reflect the qualities of the New Age of Aquarius. They are to be found in every department of human living, and are to be recognised by their altruism and keen response to human need. These are the forerunners, sent ahead to prepare men for the experiences which will characterise the New Age. Some few of them work consciously, aware of their mission to aid a struggling world and of their connection with Hierarchy, but the majority work solely from the promptings of the heart and their desire to help.

Soon, it will be obvious to many that their ideas are being echoed across the world, that a large prepared contingent is at work, voicing aloud the desire of men for change, and the implications for society that this change will inevitably bring. These changes go to the heart of the human problem today: the separation of men and nations that threatens the security of the world. Without these changes men stand on a knife-edge of disaster; the unbridled march of commercialisation into every aspect of human life endangers the race.

More and more, men are seen as superfluous in a struggle for existence, mere pawns in a gigantic game of 'hunt the dollar'. Human trust and social cohesion are nowhere to be seen in this rapacious contest for gain at any cost. Not for much longer can humanity stand the strain of this struggle, in which men are taking their stand, for love or insane greed.

Behind the scenes Maitreya and His Group fan the flames of this conflict and gradually, more and more, men are beginning to see their path. With growing will, they voice aloud their need for change, following the precepts of the men and women of vision who are leading the way.

Thus does Maitreya work for the good of all, fostering the best that men can offer and showing the best that men can become. Hierarchy looks benevolently on this momentous struggle for the future of mankind, certain of the outcome: the overcoming of both greed and despair, and the triumph of the human spirit.

6 June 2012

SI July/August 2012

Further thoughts on Unity

With the exception of a few, most of the nations of the world are seeking Unity. Their actions may not always support this statement, but inwardly, at least, the general direction of their intention is to achieve, together with their friends and allies, the expression of Unity.

However, there are some nations for whom the achievement of their individual goals is more important than general world Unity, the guarantee of world peace. These attitudes can, and sometimes do, change suddenly, or over time, but in the present period one can discuss the following countries.

Israel (rays: soul 3, personality 6), having usurped by terrorism the land of the Palestinian people, is now obsessed with its security to the exclusion of all other issues, including world peace. Sheltered from United Nations resolutions by the US Security Council veto, Israel swaggers in the Middle East without restraint. Thanks to the United States, Israel possesses the nuclear bomb and threatens its use against Iran if necessary. The people of Israel are old but the nation is very young, bold and inclined to recklessness.

The USA (rays: soul 2, personality 6) has, from the soul level, a profound and genuine desire for world Unity and peace. However, it too is young, large and powerful, and under the control of its glamoured personality. Its ideal is for Unity and peace, and it imagines that it demonstrates this to the world. When all follow the Americans' lead in economics, politics and religion, it believes, peace will inevitably ensue. With this attitude it has sought to dominate the world, repeatedly making war in the name of peace (Korea, Vietnam, Iraq, Afghanistan). The world is waiting for the overcoming of this glamour and the influence of the 2nd-ray soul of the US to emerge in world affairs.

When this does take place (probably not before the Day of Declaration by the Christ), the innate longing for Unity of the American soul will be galvanised into action, and the idea of service to the whole will replace the present need to dominate. A great reconstruction of the world will be undertaken by countless individuals. The desire to serve will replace the present US sense of superiority in all things, and a true era of peace will follow.

Iran has an ancient and gifted people, at present torn between desire for a sane, secular government and an extreme, fanatical form of Islamic rule. Iran is deeply disliked and mistrusted by the USA, since its scientists are in the process of mastering nuclear technology. It has never been the intention of Iran to develop a nuclear arsenal but it feels threatened daily by the USA and Israel and now, reluctantly, sees no alternative. The rays of Iran are soul 2, personality 4. Its people are mature, cultured and peaceful and have given much of its gifts, in particular to India.

North Korea (rays: soul 6, personality 4), is the youngest of all these nations, formed out of a division of the original Korea. Its intentions are also the most difficult to foresee, since it is so engrossed in proving to the world its prowess. Unfortunately it has achieved some nuclear capability and can be seen as something of a loose cannon among the nations. As is well known, it is dominated, rather than led, by its rulers and must be carefully watched by the United Nations as a whole. Its people are hungry, for recognition and for food. The nations should be generous in sharing both with North Korea.

From the point of view of the average on-looker there seems much to cause fear and worry in this appraisal. However, the Masters see a world ready for change, longing for the justice which will guarantee a new and real Unity among the nations, and the peace which all desire.

12 August 2012
SI September 2012

S.O.P. — Save Our Planet!

When one looks deeply into the present situation in the world, two things stand out as particularly important: the danger of war and the acceleration of the Earth's ecological imbalance. There are, of course, many other problems: the economic debacle which affects many countries, especially in the West; the huge increases in the price of food, especially the staple diet of many millions; the huge, and growing, disparity in living standards between the rich and the poor.

All of these problems are important and require early resolution. The two first named must command the attention of all sensible men and governments for they present the greatest threat to man's well-being. Wars, large and small, should by now be unthinkable, but, sadly, this is not the case. Even a world which has known the folly and futility of war at its most terrible has still not relinquished, totally, that abomination. The governments are seduced into thinking that old ways will, after all, render up their coveted prize. The weapons of war, therefore, have become indispensable and a major trading asset. While the weapons are there they will be used. Small wars beget large wars as more countries become involved. Large nations fight by proxy through their allies and so prolong unimportant quarrels into war. This major danger must be abandoned by all nations. It threatens the very existence of men on Earth.

Apart from war, nothing so profoundly affects the future of all men as much as pollution. Some countries have recognised this fact and have taken some steps to limit pollution and global warming. Others, sometimes the chief polluters, deny the reality of global warming despite the overwhelming evidence to the contrary. Daily, now, the climatic changes prove beyond doubt that the planet is sick and needs immediate and skilful care to re-establish equilibrium. Time is running out for men to halt the transformation which is being daily wrought on planet Earth. Every man, woman and child must play their part in the task. Time is, verily, running out. S.O.P. Save Our Planet!

8 September 2012
SI October 2012

[Readers may be interested to note that it is hoped that S.O.P. will eventually become an internationally well-known phrase to rally all to take action to save our planet.]

From Pisces to Aquarius

Within the present era there are many things which must be preserved, for we must not forget that the Age of Pisces, now fast fading into history, has bequeathed to us much of value and worth. Of course, the great quality of Individuality can be cited as the glory of Pisces, but there are other gifts owed to the Piscean experience of the last 2,000 years.

A new and more potent idealism has enriched the hearts and minds of millions, thus causing the birth and spread of the world's great religions with their essentially nourishing and civilising thought. The urge to know, to travel and to trade flourished as never before, and a new world, literally, appeared to men's astonished eyes. Inevitably, early trade became greedy exploitation and annexation; thus, as always, the empires grew and waxed rich and strong. Often, the conquering heroes felt – wrongly, but sometimes rightly – that they had a civilising and enlightening mission, that the "savages" needed "saving", and the gold and spices were not the real reason for their presence far from home. This was indeed so in many cases. The urge to know and to apply that knowledge is evident in the work of Leonardo Da Vinci, whose scientific explorations have led to the advance of modern medicine and even to modern aircraft and space exploration. All of this and more results from the Piscean experience.

If individuality was Pisces' greatest gift, today as we enter the new Age of Aquarius, the misuse of that same individuality has become man's greatest danger and threat. Throughout the world, powerful individuals, governments and institutions hold millions in thrall. In these circumstances, men have become pawns, held at ransom to the vagaries of the market. Institutions of all kinds – governments, banks and corporations – have reduced the shining individuality of their workers to passive obedience. Elsewhere, others starve and die in silence, or slave for a daily pittance, while the rich add riches to their unholy hoard.

This divisive norm is driving men to the edge of destruction and presents them with a historic choice: to continue thus and end, for ever, man's sojourn on Planet Earth or to change direction completely. Already, the signs are there that men have seen the danger and, throughout the world, are awakening to a new dawn. The shining light of Aquarius is entering their hearts, and the cries of justice and freedom rise readily to their lips. This same justice through sharing will bring men out of their darkness and lift them onwards to their destined goal. Thus shall it be.

13 October 2012
SI November 2012

Some thoughts on group work

The wise man is one who studies all sides of a problem or situation before coming to conclusions and actions which could later find him much at fault. The foolish man does otherwise. The type of person who springs quickly to mind in this regard is quick to enthuse and, unfortunately, as quick to deny and reject. They lack patience and consistency of thought. They tend to hold themselves high in serious self-regard which makes them harsh in judgement of others. They are usually completely unaware of the glamour of their actions and decisions.

Such people are not intrinsically useless to a group. Indeed, if events are favourable, they can be useful co-workers in many ways. However, when events run counter to their expectations, they can become very destructive and difficult to deal with. There are many such in the groups around the world who threaten the precious unity of the whole.

A common problem in the working groups is the one who does very little of the group endeavour and for that very reason plagues the group with constant criticism. They feel angry and envious that others do more, and more useful, work but are not prepared to sacrifice their time to do likewise. Their constant stream of criticism, they seldom realise, is deeply destructive of group unity and wellbeing.

Then there are those who promise their time and energy, but find, all too often, that they cannot fulfil their offer after all. Many are the stratagems of such half-hearted, half-involved people who dip their timid toes into the stern waters of true group work. This, ideally, comes from the soul, and where the soul is concerned, the work, however arduous, is welcomed and joyful, not a burden or sacrifice but a simple act of service eagerly given.

5 November 2012
SI December 2012

The importance of Unity

When men look back at this time, they will see it as a time when we displayed, simultaneously, every aspect of our being, both accomplishments and faults. This, of course, is not surprising, for men everywhere stand at various points on the evolutionary ladder but, accepting these natural divisions, which time itself will reduce, there is lacking, still, a unity of approach and an understanding of the needs of all.

Why should this be so? For long ages the teachings of successive religions and the eminence of powerful individuals sustained a certain unity of thought in evolving humanity. There were, of course, many periods of war and dissent but at some level the unifying influence of the great religions was maintained. Today, individuality is so potent, so valued and rewarded, that, despite its manifold achievements, this precious individuality has become man's greatest danger.

Unity in any real sense is all but vanquished, even, or perhaps especially, in the religious field. Few there are who see instinctively, as a matter of course, the essential needs of all men. Therein lies the danger.

The civilising forces of Justice and Freedom, however, are awakening millions to their birthright. Little by little, the minds of men are turning to the needs of all. This, naturally, runs counter to the rousing call of individuality. Hence the present extraordinary tension and chaotic conditions in the world. The problems, political and economic, are basically of a spiritual nature but can be solved only in the political and economic fields. Unity must be sought and manifested. Otherwise the strains imposed by the present conditions would drive men to the most dangerous actions. For this reason Maitreya calls for Unity, an understanding of the needs of all.

Peace is essential but can only be achieved where Justice reigns. Justice, it will be found, needs the calm waters of Trust for its achievement. Sharing alone is Maitreya's remedy for our ills. Sharing alone will bring men, trusting, to the table where Justice will be achieved and Peace assured.

12 January 2013
SI January/February 2013

Humanity's historic choice

The time for men to make their historic choice has arrived. Soon, men will come to realize that they must make a momentous decision, one which will determine the future for every man, woman and child, indeed the future for every living creature on Earth: a choice between continuous and ever expanding creativity on planet Earth, or a devastating ending of all life, human and sub-human, on our planetary home.

Man, unfortunately, has discovered the secret of the awful power which lies hidden in the nucleus of the atom and has harnessed it for war. While humanity is so separated by competition, greed and lust for power, the danger of extinction, by accident or design, is ever present. Men must therefore find a safer way to live.

So potent today is the individuality of men and nations, so divided have they become in their struggle for life, that they have lost their way and must quickly find it to survive.

Thus the Great Ones, your Elder Brothers, have sought to show the only way to peace. Only sharing and justice, We say, will bring the peace which, in their hearts, all men desire. Simple indeed is Our recommendation but, so far, difficult for humanity to grasp. Men have divine free will and are the masters of their fate. Take, We advise, the path of sharing and justice which are the garments of Brotherhood, without which a man is not fully a man.

8 February 2013
SI March 2013

The Masters' role

For many years, We, the Masters, have been preparing Ourselves for the time of Emergence, the time, now near, when We will, in group formation, live openly in the everyday world. For Some it will be an experience altogether new. Many, as Masters, have spent all Their time within the Hierarchy and must now learn to work in entirely new ways. Even the use of speech has to be learned and practised, since telepathy has long been the mode used by Us.

At first, and for some considerable time, Our contact will have to be restricted to senior disciples in the various fields of work and to trained personnel involved in the practical fields of administration, especially in food distribution. Many Masters are specialists in administration, while Others engage more readily in teaching. The aim is to work as closely as possible in every field, and as soon as possible with the general public. It is important to emphasise that the Masters' aim is to stimulate and guide humanity as needed, but to safeguard the essential freewill of men.

Gradually the location of the various Mystery Schools, preparatory and advanced, will become known and many thousands of striving disciples will gravitate to them. There they will receive the training for the first two initiations, and enter the Sanctuary of Hierarchy.

In the beginning We must expect some opposition to the Masters' presence and ideas, but eventually, even the most diehard fundamentalist of any religion or creed will find it difficult to fault the harmlessness of man's Elder Brothers.

In due course, the cities of the world will be beautified and transformed. The new Science of Light will transform industry and travel, and the movement of people will bring

Unity to the world. People of all nations will work and team together in service to all. The advice of the Masters will be available, guiding men wisely with a gentle hand.

The presence of even a few Masters among them will have an electrifying effect on thousands of people anxious to serve the needs of the world, and the idea of service will become a new life aim for many. In this way it can be seen that an enormous transformation can be accomplished in a relatively very short period of time. A mass programme of aid to the poor will achieve miracles in countries in Africa and South America, for example. An altogether new sense of the need for haste to rectify the wrongs of the past will ensure an intensity of help unknown today. Inspired by Maitreya and His group, hundreds of thousands of men and women will find their vocation in this way.

We, the Masters, aim only to teach and guide, to show the way for men and protect them from harm. War in all its forms must become a thing of the past but the decision to make it so must be man's alone. I repeat, Our task is to show the way, to outline the plans, but men alone must embrace each step of the way. Have no fear; all will be achieved. The life ahead for men could not be more bright.

9 March 2013
SI April 2013

The aspiration of the young

It will not surprise any intelligent reader to learn that, in Our estimation, the present chaotic economic and resultant social conditions will not last for very much longer. Nor do We see a sudden transformation and return to the mythical 'status quo'. The peoples of the world, in millions, have begun to sense the aroma of freedom, and for little longer will be denied its boon.

Across the world, most especially among the young, the potent desire for change is being given expression. The young want a new kind of world, a new structure which includes them and their aspirations. These aspirations are for justice and sharing, for meaningful work and an opportunity to raise their families in sufficiency and peace. For too long have they languished in poverty and obscurity, denied a say in their life's endeavour.

From now on the governments of the world will have to consider seriously these aspirations of the hitherto silent majority, and change their plans accordingly. The 'landed rich' will find it difficult to maintain the dramatic gap between their way of life and that of the average 'peasant', as the cry for equality forces change. It will be understood that the present divisions in financial power are central to the instability of world finance.

The old order is collapsing and no government can halt this process. The new energies of Aquarius are waxing stronger, breaking asunder the old corrupt and decadent order. The young, and young at heart, are the first to register the appearance of this new aspiration for justice. The desire for right relationship wells up strongly in the hearts of the young.

Meanwhile Maitreya continues His progress among the nations, speaking freely of the need for justice, sharing and love. These ideas are finding many followers as the tension of today's conditions makes its impact throughout the world. In the USA and Mexico, in Brazil and now in Russia, Maitreya places before His audiences the alternatives facing humanity: to continue on the present senseless and greedy path to oblivion or to see the world as one, on a journey to perfection, as brothers and sisters; to see that only sharing and justice will give us the peace we all desire and a world that prospers according to the Plan, and so find our way back to the Truth and Beauty we once knew and fostered.

8 April 2013
SI May 2013

Whither now?

It is becoming more and more obvious that the economic systems of today no longer work. Too many, millions indeed, are excluded from the right to sufficient food to sustain life. The productive capacity of this planet is vast, but so inadequate and unequal are the means of distribution that millions suffer and die without cause. Men know this to be true yet little is done to remedy this crime.

Whither now? For how much longer must the poor suffer in this way? For how long can the nations support this iniquity before an immeasurable catastrophe engulfs the world?

Is it not strange that men have never sought to remedy this eternal, tragic situation where millions suffer and die from want in the midst of plenty? The simplest of solutions, it would seem, has never occurred to those who have abundant plenty. Why does not simple justice reveal the solution? That the rich must share the riches they control is not only sensible and just but essential for world peace and the benefit of all if the survival of all is to be assured.

Make no mistake, men must come to realise that sharing is not simply a good and just idea but is essential if mankind is to survive. Only wise and just sharing will bring the peace which all men desire. For without sharing trust would never arise.

Be assured that Maitreya Himself will tell men this simple truth and open their eyes to the benefits which will follow. Become one of His many workers who seek to establish the need for sharing and justice. Remember that no man is separate and alone, that all men, knowingly or not, are linked together with invisible ties in a long journey of succeeding revelation. Renounce the path of separation and aid your brothers and sisters on the way.

9 May 2013
SI June 2013

The people's voice heralds the future

It is becoming more and more obvious to many that the present economic structure of the world is in tatters and must be changed. For example, the economies of the USA, Europe and Japan are in the doldrums; and China, so recently the powerhouse, is slowing down. Only India, where millions still live and die in poverty, and Brazil hold aloft the banner of 'success'.

Admittedly, this is a very partial view of the economies of the world but it is largely the case that the nations are languishing and know not how to prosper. The old tricks no longer work: university graduates feel lucky to serve in bars; the poor are poorer than ever and are thankful for food banks; the middle classes struggle to 'keep up'; the rich are richer than ever but believe they are over-taxed. Governments try, but their priorities are mistaken and their methods no longer are relevant to the problems which face the world.

The people, however, who suffer most from government inaction or wrong thinking, see clearly their own needs. They look for freedom, justice, the right to work and a world at peace in which their families can thrive. Their demands are more and more being given voice. For little longer will the mass of men restrain the anger and frustration which is their lot. They trust no longer the words or the actions of governments done in their name. For too long, and too often, they have been deceived and cheated of their birthright. They see this in simple terms but with clear eyes, trusting no longer the machinations of the powerful rich. The voice of the people is rising, nay, has risen, and is calling men to declare themselves.

The people, clear-eyed and unafraid, have looked into the future and have seen the possibility of the fulfilment of their aspirations for a just and peaceful world. They know that this will not happen by itself but that they must, together with their brothers and sisters, take the power of fulfilment into their own hands. They know too that the way may be hard and dangerous but that the prize is too precious for them to fail, for it is the prize of brotherhood, of justice and peace, and a better, simpler and truer life for all. They know that no sacrifice is too great for this achievement and are willing to die in its name.

Thus will the people of the world inherit the birthright of freedom and justice that is their due. Thus will the voice of the people rise louder and clearer in the months and years ahead.

6 June 2013
SI July/August 2013

The twin pillars of the future

From now on, the 'makers and shakers' of this world, the men of wealth and power, will find a growing resistance to their stratagems and plans. In response to the growing influence of the beneficent energies of Aquarius, there is emerging the awareness of a different form of living in which all can benefit and grow, and manifest their talents and ideas for the greater good of all.

There is, too, a growing sense that money is not, after all, a god and demands no devotion or obeisance; that money is but a tool, to use or not, a convenience which has become a tyrant that enslaves its masters.

From now on, too, it will become increasingly evident that the old forms and methods no longer work, certainly not for the benefit of more than a few. Thus a great divide has opened up between the rich and poor of every nation, sharper and clearer than ever before. For little longer will the poor of this world accept this unsacred division. And so the threat of revolution stirs once more in many countries. In Our view, while understandable, such a consequence would not bode well for humanity and would but strengthen their despair.

Our way is the way of peaceful evolution, and we recommend it to those who would endanger further the world. Our way is simple and attainable; the principle of sharing is the blessed answer to men's ills. At a stroke Just Sharing will transform this world. Many other ways have been tried and have failed. Is it not a wonder that sharing has never found a place in the plans of men?

Maitreya, even now, speaks daily of the need for Sharing and Justice, the twin pillars of the new society of Peace and Reconciliation. Hold firmly therefore to this simple path and bring joy to the hearts of all.

9 August 2013
SI September 2013

Humanity awakes

One day soon it will be realised by many that the Christ, or someone similar, is living among us. So great has been the response to the interviews on television which Maitreya has given so far that a powerful thoughtform is emerging: the belief that the Blessed Time has arrived when the Teacher of Old has returned. This expectation is now sweeping through the world.

In many countries, Brazil, China and Russia, for example, there is a growing sense that very soon the world will awaken to the news that the Teacher is here, or on His way. This phenomenon is due, of course, to the impact of Maitreya's appearances on television so far, and to the faithful work of preparation carried out by the dedicated groups throughout the world.

This news should encourage these steadfast servers to continue their efforts and, if possible, to redouble them. We, your Elder Brothers, are well aware of the strain which this long effort has imposed on the groups, and commend their work over many years. That effort, it will soon be known, has not been in vain.

From now on, those engaged in the work of preparation should find a greater openness and readiness to believe that the advent of the Teacher is imminent; that the people are ready for change; that a new world is in the making; and that sharing and justice, freedom and joy await all men.

3 September 2013
SI October 2013

The dynamics of change

If men could see the extraordinary happenings which are taking place today in many parts of the world, they would realise that the Day of Declaration cannot be too far off. They would see thousands of people marching and calling for change, for a better life and a new approach to living: one that will guarantee them work and food for their families, needed healthcare and a say in their own future.

Many are the plans now being drawn which articulate these ideas; groups and individuals worldwide are formulating the blueprint of a new world. Some are too hysterical to be taken seriously, but many are well thought out and offer worthwhile proposals to bring about the needed changes.

We, your Elder Brothers, are much encouraged by these events, showing eloquently how ready are men for change. Of course, there are many still who are afraid of the future and terrified of change, but the forces of transformation are now so potent that change will come to the people, ready or not.

Throughout the world these forces of transformation are compelling millions to see a better life ahead: one that will install peace, justice and sharing to the rightful place in their lives.

We, too, have Our plans, which will be presented to men. The free will of men will never be usurped and the speed of adoption of these plans will follow this law. Thus will a transformation of life on Earth take place with a minimum of disruption. Each step will be vetted by men, so that humanity itself will regulate the speed of change.

That not all are ready for such transformation cannot be denied, but so great is the necessity for new and more peaceful ways of living that change must come, step by step, in ordered sequence. Only in this way can catastrophe be averted.

When the doubters see the benefits that will come by this method they will gladly accept the new calm and harmony which will descend on Earth.

10 October 2013

SI November 2013

A blueprint for sharing

When men consider the principle of sharing, they almost always see it in personal terms. They visualize a situation in which they, personally, will be expected to give away considerable sums of money to far-off people whom they do not know, nor care to know. In fact, the principle of sharing can only be organized as a global process.

There are several ways in which this could be achieved, either partially or totally. We, your Elder Brothers, consider that the following is the most practical, the simplest and fairest method of all, one which, if adopted, would satisfy the greatest number. Each nation, We suggest, would be asked to make an inventory of all their resources and needs, what they produce themselves and what they are obliged to import. Then, each nation would be asked to put into a common pool that which they have in excess of their needs, forming a huge international resource from which all could draw. Naturally, the large developed nations would give a greater amount but all would donate their un-needed surplus. This scheme appeals to us for its simplicity and fairness; it would, of course, take time to implement, but We foresee a time when it can be accomplished.

Many are the trained organizers and administrators for whom this work would provide a welcome service to the world. All would proceed under the aegis of a Master or at least a third-degree initiate, to safeguard the trust of all. Thus, at a stroke the curse of poverty and want would be ended. The hearts and lives of countless millions would be lifted into joy, and those who shared for the first time would find a happiness deep and satisfying, which perhaps, they were afraid to know.

In this way only would be engendered the trust essential for the ending of war and terrorism. Without such trust there will never be peace. Without peace the future for mankind would be bleak indeed. Therefore, some form of sharing is essential if we are to survive. When the majority of men realize this, the major problems of the world can be solved.

The principle of sharing is beginning to enter the minds of many groups throughout the world. Bit by bit men inch their way to this conclusion. Maitreya reminds all who hear Him that sharing alone provides the solution to our troubles. Thus, as the weeks and months go by, men can be seen to grapple with their problems, and more and more find sharing to be the key to their future.

5 November 2013
SI December 2013

The coming joy of Aquarius

When men look back at this time, they will wonder in disbelief at the atrocities and suffering they have tolerated for so long. Some will blame and call for punishment and settling of scores. Maitreya, men will find, will caution otherwise. Justice, like sharing and freedom, is divine, He will attest. Retribution is not His way, and leads men back to the past.

When men realize this, they will abandon their longing for revenge and, inspired by Maitreya and His group of Masters, they will tackle the tremendous task of transformation with zeal.

The changes needed, of course, are vast and will have their priorities. Millions now starving and living in penury, or the dislocation of war, will be the first to be released from agony. The principle of Sharing, on whose divine justice the future of this planet rests, will take pride of place. When men take stock of this accomplishment, they will wonder, sadly, why the principle of Sharing took so long to enter their hearts.

Thus will men grow in stature as they contemplate their past errors in the light of the new achievements. Thus will quicken their determination to fashion a new world from a fast fading past.

The Masters will inspire the inauguration of a new approach to living, which all men can share and of which all can be a part. A growing sense of brotherhood and co-operation will bring a new joy to their task. As time proceeds, this new attitude to work and to each other will herald the glory that Aquarius brings.

9 January 2014
SI January/February 2014

The Path of Ascent

Within each man and woman sits a God, potential as yet but everlasting. As they go through the experiences of what we call life, they make a journey, which in the end turns out to have been a step towards oneness with that God, realizing the fact of its divinity, realizing that it is the Soul, our higher Self.

Heretofore, our knowledge of the Soul has come from religious texts. These have left man with the impression that the Soul is distant from himself, something to be recognized and worshipped from afar. As man progresses, however, he comes to understand that the Soul is himself, a higher and purer part of himself, but nevertheless himself. Thus a man progresses, deepening in knowledge of his true being and purpose.

Today, thousands of people are consciously aware of making such a journey; for them life is deepening in meaning, and they search for greater knowledge and experience. Thus, in time, they turn to meditation and through this practice a great discovery is theirs. Step by step, they know for certain that they are Souls, that the Soul is not some distant idea but their very being. Gradually the tempo of their lives changes, and a deeper meaning and purpose consolidates all that they do. Thus do men advance on the journey to perfection, reflecting more and more the divinity and wisdom of the Soul.

All in their own way make such a journey, some swiftly and eagerly, others more slowly and less sure of the path. But all eventually pass through the various gates which mark their progress on the way. Today this journey is trodden by millions who know not that the path exists but nevertheless answer the call of their Soul, and enter thereon. They sense the needs of the time and seek to meet these needs, and so play their part.

Knowingly or not they are responding to the call from Maitreya through their Souls to enter the fray, and to replenish this world with their ardour and courage. Their efforts, they will find, have not been in vain.

4 February 2014
SI March 2014

Problems awaiting action

It can be said without fear of contradiction that not all is right with the world. For example, the gap between the very rich and the hopelessly poor grows ever wider. This extreme imbalance is not healthy for any society. To be sure a few members of the rich community do indeed share their wealth with the poor, but in general the very rich aim rather at becoming mega-rich to the detriment of all.

The ever-increasing commercialization of every aspect of life today is, in itself, a 'time bomb' whose rupture will bring the present economic structure to its knees. This time is not far off. So great are the tensions caused by this deep materialism that equilibrium is strained to breaking point. Most people are unaware of these forces, so deeply involved are they in the building of the tension.

Thus will be presented to men their only natural course: the adoption of the principle of sharing. More and more, humanity is being edged towards this realization, however distant as yet are they from its actual manifestation.

At the same time the ecological problems facing the world continue to a climax. Most countries today recognize that global warming is the enemy of all. The question which divides the nations is whether and to what extent man is responsible. The wisest course that men can follow is to assume that they are responsible for most of the pressures on the climate and to take all practical measures to rectify the problems. Some nations assuredly are doing so but not all. Our advice is that the actions and non-actions of humanity are responsible for eighty per cent of the problem and that men must, for their own and their children's sake, spare nothing in its alleviation. Be assured that We will help them but they must play their part.

With the collapse of the world economy men will come to realize their oneness. This realization will have a profound effect on their attitude to war. They will see that they are bound together in a struggle for survival, and the words of Maitreya will resound more loudly in their minds. Sharing, justice and freedom will grow in men's minds as powerful symbols of the future, as inherent rights of all, the way to correct relationship.

5 March 2014
SI April 2014

Gambling gestures

Whenever men make a determined step into right relationship, there are always others who make an equally determined step into confrontation. Multitudes work, and even die, for greater freedom and justice; while other forces threaten the peace in cynical attempts to consolidate their diminishing power. Meanwhile, humanity at large watches and trembles, witnessing with fear a renewal of ancient hatred thought to be discarded and overcome.

We, your Elder Brothers, too, watch carefully this dangerous ploy, but fear not. Common sense, We know, will force the acceptance of at least a precarious peace, with gains and losses balanced, more or less.

From now on this scenario will be repeated across the world, where the 'great powers' attempt to maintain or to even increase their power, knowing, however, that they must do so carefully without damaging the status quo.

For how long can the nations play this useless game? The only sensible course is to work together for peace and prosperity for all. Only in this way will they ready their peoples for the joy of peace, the prosperity of justice, and the bliss of sharing.

3 May 2014
SI June 2014

The new environment

When the Masters begin Their historic return to the everyday world, They will find much to do to enable Them to function adequately in the new environment. As many know, telepathy is Their normal mode of communication but, working with men, They will have to learn again the long-discarded human speech. Many of your Elder Brothers are already hard at work on problems of physical plane activity. In this way, a greater degree of trust and facility of work will be engendered.

Furthermore, many Masters have had little or no direct contact with humanity for centuries and so will find the situation and mode of working altogether new. Of course, most Masters are very adaptable and quick to learn but inevitably some will find the unfamiliar experience of working on the outer planes taxing indeed.

For many years now, certain Masters have trained a large group of disciples in the difficult work of implementing the plans, political and economic, of the new civilization. These trained men and women, chosen by democratic vote, will make concrete and real the plans of the more senior members of the Hierarchy. Thus will the reconstruction of the world go forward smoothly, as the people's needs are recognized and accepted. The task of reconstruction is vast, offering men a field of service like never before. Countless millions living in poverty and want must be the first to receive a crash programme of aid on a scale never yet attempted.

Gradually our gigantic cities will give way to smaller ones with an abundance of gardens and parks. The ugly slums of today will be replaced by varied areas of stimulus and rest. One of the obvious differences will be the absence of pollution and smog. In town and country fresh air will be truly fresh. Travel will be fast and silent and the longest journeys short and pleasurable. Fatigue will disappear.

Obviously all of this will take time to implement but step by step the search for beauty will become the keynote of our existence. Free, unlimited energy, owned by all and shared by all, will guarantee this transformation. Thus will the New Age be heralded, calling all men to give of their best in service to the Plan.

31 May 2014
SI July/August 2014

The way ahead

Welcome to the feast. As we stand on the brink of the New Age, men wonder what awaits them. As many will know, the world is divided into two groups, roughly equal in number. One demonstrates the characteristics of the age of Pisces, now fading fast. The glory of that age, the powerful individuality which now demonstrates across the world, has become, today, our greatest danger, threatening the future of all. Thus the nations compete without mercy, the largest and strongest claiming the lion's share.

Daily, however, the beneficent waters of Aquarius make more their presence felt, edging man away from the abyss.

Millions now sense that man is One, that only by working together for the good of all can mankind survive.

This new and wiser concept is awakening in men everywhere, showing the way to future harmony. This awakening cannot be halted or diverted for behind it are the great Lords of Synthesis, of Blending and Fusion. Thus will be ushered in the new dispensation, the Great Lord, Maitreya Himself, leading the way.

The time is now almost upon us. Watch, and sleep not, nor miss His Call.

6 August 2014
SI September 2014

The Sword of Cleavage

Many people believe that despite the presence of Maitreya in the world, everything is becoming more threatening and unstable than hitherto. They wonder what Hierarchy is doing to ease the many problems and difficulties that leave them afraid and unprepared for the heightened tension of today.

The truth is, the world *is* being prepared. In times of great tension and change, people look at problems with a limited view – which they inevitably have – of the true state of society. Humanity imagines that all these events have the same impact and importance for the future, whereas the true view, which only the Masters can see, is altogether different. The Masters see the happenings as if occurring on a flat plane, and as potential only. They know that some will precipitate and effect world change, while others will simply wither away without any precipitation at all. Humanity, with its limited vision, sees all these events as bearing on their future but this assuredly is not the case. From the Masters' point of view humanity has never been so ready for the new world that the future will bring. It has never been so near a time of inspiration and readiness to work for the common weal.

When the Christ said that He would return (in such a time as we think not), He would bring not soft words of spurious peace but a sword, the Sword of Cleavage, which would separate father from son and brother from brother. It is precisely the action of the Sword of Cleavage that we are witnessing today. Maitreya's energy of love stimulates everyone: the one who loves, and works for justice and sharing, but also the one who causes the divisions, schisms and greed in the world. In this way, through the clear opposition created by the Sword of Cleavage, men can arrive at a true choice for the future – the future for all men, the poor and hungry as well as the men of money and the destroyers of peace in the world. Each of us must choose on which side of that division we find our truth.

6 September 2014
SI October 2014

Message from Maitreya
7 October 2014

When men see Me for the first time and know Me for what I am, they will find themselves changing inwardly.

Many will for a time return to the joy of childhood and find the world a better home thereby. Many will feel strengthened in their desire to serve and to place themselves in the forefront of change. These are the ones on whom I shall call for the task of replenishment of man's spirit and joy.

Believe if you can that I am with you, ready to use My strength on your behalf.

Believe, if you can, My friends, that I am eagerly awaiting the day of My open return.

[Readers will notice that this message is from Maitreya, the World Teacher, rather than Benjamin Creme's Master. It was given, by a process of mental telepathy through Benjamin Creme.]

SI November 2014

Call to reason

The time is soon coming when men will realize that the most important problem facing this generation is the ecological imbalance which threatens vast areas of Earth. As you know, men are divided as to the extent of this problem but unless their attention is squarely fixed on this ecological dilemma, the future for many is under question.

Soon many groups will realize the full import of this danger and that, year by year, little separates them from disaster. The forces unleashed by global warming are now well beyond the control devices available to men.

Hearken, therefore, while there is still a little time. For the waters rise inexorably, and men gamble, blithely, with their future.

S.O.P. – Save Our Planet.

8 November 2014
SI December 2014

The year ahead

Somewhere toward the end of this year people should see the beginning of a change in various areas of the world. What has been seen as harmful will in the end be seen as beneficial.

Hunger and hate together might well begin to cease to dominate the pages of our newspapers.

A quieter mood will at least begin to replace the anger and tribal ferocity of the present. Be not mistaken – this is not the end of hardship. For some there lies ahead unwelcome hardship but so it must be, for they themselves have created the situations that bring it about.

However, this will not be for long. Beneficial energies of Aquarius are hastening the process of renewal and this should be seen as the keynote of the future.

People everywhere are waiting for change and change they will have, whether welcome or otherwise.

Have no fear for all is for the best.

12 January 2015
SI January/February 2015

Advent of the new

The time immediately ahead will puzzle many, so quick will be the changes, political, economic and social, which will manifest, and so frequently will these changes occur.

For many, anxiety and puzzlement will be the major response. Intrigued or alarmed by the nature and extent of these changes, many will see them as signs of a transforming society, while others will fear and resent the new manifestation. People everywhere will act warily, unsure of the right direction for them to take.

Not for long, however, will men act thus. They will find that it is a truly changing world in which they live, beset with greater challenges to their beliefs and values.

Thus will men begin to establish the new out of the old, and to demonstrate their growing ability to respond to the challenges of the time.

8 February 2015
SI March 2015

The justice of the Law

Men live in a changing world and must accept it as the norm. For some, these changes will seem threatening and unwelcome while for others, especially the young, they will be welcomed with open arms. Be assured that they are for the best, whatever your stance, for they reflect the needs of the time, and are inevitable and just.

Men should realize that they themselves are creating the conditions whereby these changes impact their lives. When this realism bears fruit, a smoother transition into the new time will become the norm.

Our advice to men is this: hold not to blaming unseen forces but realize your own part in creating the transformations of our time. Be assured that out of these transformations will come an ecstatic joy.

8 March 2015
SI April 2015

Signs of the new

Soon it will become clear to men that signs they look for are appearing. For some these signs will seem inevitable and welcome. For others they will seem like the dissolution of all that they hold dear. In truth, they will be the signs that denote the new, and are but the outer expression of profound changes that are taking place. In time, most will agree that much was wrong in the old world, now quickly passing out, and had to be sacrificed for the better expression of man's nature and accomplishments.

Soon, therefore, the changes heralded by these signs will alert the keen-eyed of men that we are entering a new dispensation, one of which all can be proud.

11 April 2015
SI May 2015

A gift from the Highest

Men stand at a point of revelation, which soon will sweep away discordant voices and attitudes. They will know more keenly the meaning and purpose of their existence, and the means by which that knowledge is brought into their awareness. Soon, very soon now men will grow, overnight as it were.

This new knowledge will chasten and surprise many but inspire and enlighten them into a complete adjustment of their understanding. This will give a new value to what they call the meaning and purpose of life. A greater seriousness and a greater joy will permeate their beliefs and actions, and gradually involve them all together in a new dispensation. That time is not far off. The Great Lord is eager to appear and to grace the world by His open, recognized presence.

Have no fear. A new world is in the making, which will restore men's faith and courage in equal order.

10 May 2015
SI June 2015

The onslaught of the new

For some people the coming months will feel to be the most difficult they have known, causing them to search for even a glimmer of hope, of respite from forces with which they feel unable to cope.

At the same time, for others, there will be a heightened sense of their ingenuity and creativity, however unreal this may be. All is moving swiftly into the New Age and impress of Aquarius, whatever the 'reading' of this event. The impact of this will be powerful indeed.

How then should men respond? Know this as a further step towards the New Time and in doing so await the appearance of the Great Lord. Open the gates of heart and mind and be prepared for the onslaught of the new.

16 June 2015
SI July/August 2015

The world is ready

Soon, very soon now, men will realize the power that lies unused in their hands. They will see that they have the ability to change the quality of their lives. They are beginning to understand that freedom, justice and right relationship, one to another, are essential for man's living. Many are calling for the structures which will ensure the creation of this blessed state.

This makes clear to Maitreya that the world is ready for the new dispensation. Men should, therefore, use the limited time available to make known His presence and so prepare His way.

7 September 2015
SI October 2015

On the terrorist attack
in Paris on 13 November

Painful as it has been for the people of France the recent tragic event in Paris has opened the way for Maitreya to act sooner than would otherwise have been the case. Tragic as it is for so many it has released His Hands. Remember this and be ready for His manifestation.

14 November 2015
SI December 2015

Welcome to the New Time

Welcome, welcome to the New Time, the New Age of Oneness. Many today are frightened by the onset of the New Age, but let them look carefully at what is happening and they will see the coming together of some of the most gifted exponents of change.

Currently there is in the world a group of wise individuals showing humanity the new situation. Among others, Pope Francis is a unique expression of the people's ideal, and close to his people. The Dalai Lama, too, is playing a powerful role on behalf of the people he represents.

Never before has such a group of gifted representatives been gathered together at one time to show humanity that all is well, and that men everywhere have little time to wait to see the fulfilment of their dreams. They bless each day that passes and brings their love close to the hearts of men everywhere.

Love them too in return and embrace them in the name of the Coming One. Turn your fears into loving expectation and await the new time in the bliss which is yours by right. It is not long, not long until you see the wonder of His face, until you know the joy of His presence and His love for all. Then you will know why you are in incarnation at this special time.

God bless you and forever banish your fears.

14 January 2016
SI January/February 2016

Message from Maitreya

31 March 2016

These days are difficult for many. Even the best and the closest feel the pains of doubt and reservation.

But when I say that I engage with you as one of you before the world, it is the truth.

Likewise when I say that the time is close indeed when *all* men will recognize My face and respond, it is the truth.

Only the Law bids Me wait a very little time, but within the Law I am verily with you daily, in constant rapport with your needs and the opportunities presented to Myself by you.

Soon humanity as a whole will awaken to My presence and will accept with all willingness the transformation of this, our world.

Remember that we are at the beginning and the end of a civilization, an epic period in the history of the world, and understand thereby that men feel the pain of change.

For some it is a release into freedom. For others it is a loss of surety and calm.

But, My brothers, pain will be short-lived, and already many know this to be so. There is aid in abundance to help you through these difficult times. Accept eagerly this Age and recognize the signs of the new.

Verily, verily, I am with you. Verily, I am among you in many ways.

Judge for yourselves, My brothers, how close you are to My expectations of a new world. This will be a world in which all men are one, in which all men fulfil the joy of creation, and fulfil with love their capacity to show the way to their brothers in simplicity and truth.

SI May 2016

[Readers will notice that this message is from Maitreya, the World Teacher, rather than Benjamin Creme's Master.]

Master's comment on the current world crisis

The present situation will soon turn for the better. The storm is nearly over. It is losing its intensity, even if we do not, as yet, recognize it.

Turmoil is almost always the result of the change from one Cosmic state to another. Many people are still enmeshed in the old ways. Many people are too worried or too unaware to recognize the need for another way of acting and being.

It is also a question of how humanity responds to the new energies. Most of the response is based on greed or fear. The wealthy have become independent and very greedy. They are afraid they will not be able to take advantage of everything on offer; they are also afraid of losing their wealth. Men have to realize that the world is One – One humanity. The rich, who manage the resources based on greed and competition, deny this truth at their peril.

25 July 2016
SI September 2016

Special statement by the Master

The difficult times are all but over and people should await confidently the New Time, when Maitreya will demonstrate His high Being and all will acknowledge Him as the Master for this time.

5 October 2016
SI December 2016

[This is the last statement received from the Master through Benjamin Creme.]

ADDENDUM

Messages from Maitreya, 2000 to 2010

This special section contains Messages from Maitreya received through Benjamin Creme by a process of mental telepathy, during his interviews between 2000 and 2010.

Message from Maitreya, *14 December 2000*
My friends, very little time will elapse before you see Me. May you respond quickly and heartily to My words. Be not afraid in the times immediately ahead for they are the precursors of the happiest time of your lives.

Your interest in My story is welcomed, but believe Me, it is not a story. It is a reality which one day you will tell your children, and they shall tell theirs, and so on, for many, many years. I shall live among you as your brother and teacher and release in you that awareness to which we give the name of God. My blessings now are all around you. Be happy and wait patiently for My emergence truly.

SI January/February 2001
(Received at the end of Benjamin Creme's interview for a documentary on UK's Channel 4 Television, London, UK)

Message from Maitreya, *29 July 2002*
My friends, you will see Me very soon. Some of you are afraid of My coming, but I say to you, be not afraid, for I love you, each one, now and always. My heart is filled with God's love for you all.

SI October 2002

(Received at the end of Benjamin Creme's interview by Frank Sontag on Radio KLOS's 'Impact' show, USA)

Message from Maitreya, *20 March 2003*
There is little time to wait, now, until you see My face. Be of good cheer amid the strain of the present circumstances. Keep high your hopes of a better future for all. My Heart is filled with God's Love. This Love I send to all who hear Me.

SI May 2003

(Received at the end of Benjamin Creme's interview on Radio Ici & Maintenant, Paris, France.)

Message from Maitreya, *15 April 2004*
My Friends, I am not far from your lives. Every thought and every aspiration finds its recognition in Me. Look for Me as a simple man with answers to your profound and difficult questions. Search your hearts for the ways of love and make them manifest.
I have come into your lives not too soon, not too late, but timely. Look for Me, then, in the immediate future, and if I touch your hearts, follow Me.

SI June 2004

(Received at the end of Benjamin Creme's interview on Radio Ici & Maintenant, Paris, France.)

Message from Maitreya, 23 September 2004
Wait for me a little longer only, and you will find your dreams fulfilled. So will it be, and soon My nourishing Love will strengthen and invest your life with joy.

SI November 2004

(Received at the end of Benjamin Creme's television interview in Amsterdam, the Netherlands.)

Message from Maitreya, *6 April 2006*

My friends, I am nearer to you than you may think. My heart beats step by step with yours. My heart cries for the suffering of so many. Yet I know that the hearts of those who hear Me now are open and willing to help. Fear not My friends. Give bravely and willingly to help all in need. When you do this you enter that area of divinity from which you come. This is the action of divinity itself.

So My friends, wait no longer for the manifestation of the great changes which are to come. Bring them about by your actions. Think widely. Think that your brothers and sisters are yourselves, the same throughout the world. Do this My friends and see Me very soon. My heart embraces you all.

SI May 2006
(Received at the end of Benjamin Creme's interview on Radio Ici & Maintenant, Paris, France.)

Message from Maitreya, *29 December 2006*

I am closer to you than you may think. No distance separates us. And I can tell you truly that it is not long before you see My face. Be arderous in the task of telling the world of My presence and bring joy to humankind. Goodnight, My friends.

SI January/February 2007
(Received at the end of Benjamin Creme's interview with Bill Maher for the documentary film Religulous.)

Message from Maitreya, *27 September 2007*

My dear friends, I am close to you now. Many of you have awaited My presence for a long time. I am about to step forward openly before all men, and to begin my outer mission. There is no distance between us. Know this. Understand this. When you ask Me through the 'hand'* or directly to Me for help, that help, you should know, is assured. It is possible that you will not recognize that the help has been given, but so it will be. Trust Me to aid you, for it is to do so that I come. I shall exhort you to work with Me for the good of all. This is the opportunity to grow quicker, faster than you have ever done before, and so bring you to the Feet of That One Whom we call God. Be not afraid of the many problems which arise now almost daily in the world. These events are transient and soon men will come to understand that they have before them a future bathed in light. So will it be.

SI November 2007
(Received at the end of Benjamin Creme's interview for a television documentary in Amsterdam, the Netherlands.)

* Maitreya refers to His own hand print — see page 239

Message from Maitreya, *27 March 2008*
I am close to you indeed My friends. I am so near to you that you have but little time to wait to see Me.

Many of you have been very patient, but the timing of My approach to you and the world is governed by many laws, and I come at the earliest possible moment.

Look for Me then sooner than you think possible. Perhaps not tomorrow, or next week, or even next month, but very, very soon.

My heart is filled with the urge to complete this great endeavour. This will need the assistance of all who love their fellow men. Men must save the world which ails badly. My Masters and I will show the way to do so.

It gladdens Our hearts to see the start already made by the ordinary people of the world. It is to them I speak now.

Raise your voices. Tell the world your needs: your need for peace; your need for justice and freedom; the need for all people to live in harmony, no matter the religion, the colour, the race.

All men essentially are One. They are My brothers and I love each one.

My blessing of love flows to you all. Until soon My friends.

SI May 2008
(Received at the end of Benjamin Creme's interview on Radio Ici & Maintenant, Paris, France.)

Message from Maitreya, *26 October 2008*
My friends, listen carefully for I bring hope to you all for an end to your troubles, for a new life for all those ready to accept the need for justice and peace. [The lack of] these two, justice and peace, is the major obstacle in your path today. The way to justice and peace is easily solved. It requires only the acceptance of sharing. Share and know the future. Refuse to share and there will be no future for man.

Simple is life when seen with the knowing eye.

Learn, My friends, to live simply and to love one another truly.

My friends, believe it to be true for so it is, that you shall see Me sooner than you can imagine.

I am even now at the door, ready to step forward and to begin My more open Mission.

Be hopeful and of good cheer, My friends, for all will be well. All manner of things will be well.

SI December 2008
(Received while Benjamin Creme was filmed for Slovenian television in Munich, Germany.)

Message from Maitreya, *26 March 2010*
Give Me the opportunity to help you; that is why I have

come. If you accept Me I will lead you into your destiny; that which has been destined from the beginning of this world.

All depends on you: you have to take the steps which make this possible.

We have to see ourselves as One, brothers and sisters, and work together for the good of all.

We are not separate, despite appearances, we are one group of which I am part, and for whom I work every moment of My Life.

I would have you know that at this moment My Blessing is upon you. Accept My Blessing, and live simply and with love.

These qualities are close to My Heart.

SI May 2010

(Received at the end of Benjamin Creme's interview on Radio Ici & Maintenant, Paris, France.)

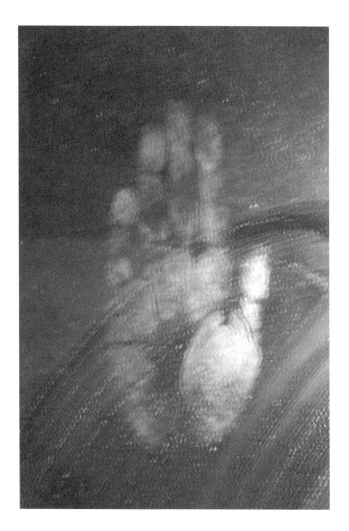

The 'hand' of Maitreya

Maitreya miraculously manifested his 'handprint' on a bathroom mirror in Barcelona, Spain, in September 2001. It is a means of invoking the healing energies and help of Maitreya, the World Teacher, who says: *"My help is yours to command, you have only to ask."*

TRANSMISSION MEDITATION

A brief explanation

A group meditation providing both a dynamic service to the world and powerful, personal spiritual development.

Transmission Meditation is a group meditation established better to distribute spiritual energies from their Custodians, the Masters of Wisdom, our planetary Spiritual Hierarchy. It is a means of 'stepping down' (transforming) these energies so that they become accessible and useful to the general public. It is the creation, in co-operation with the Hierarchy of Masters, of a vortex or pool of higher energy for the benefit of humanity.

In March 1974, under the direction of his Master, Benjamin Creme formed the first Transmission Meditation group in London. Today there are hundreds of Transmission Meditation groups around the world and new groups are forming all the time.

Transmission Meditation groups provide a link whereby Hierarchy can respond to world need. The prime motive of this work is service, but it also constitutes a powerful mode of personal growth. Many people are searching for ways in which to improve the world; this desire to serve can be strong, but difficult, in our busy lives, to fulfil. Our soul needs a means to serve, but we do not always respond to its call, and so produce disequilibrium and conflict within ourselves. Transmission Meditation provides a unique opportunity for service in a potent and fully scientific way with the minimum expenditure of one's time and energy.

Benjamin Creme held Transmission Meditation workshops around the world. During the meditation he was overshadowed by Maitreya, the World Teacher, which allowed Maitreya to confer great spiritual nourishment on the participants. Many people are inspired to begin Transmission Meditation after attending such a workshop, and many acknowledge having received healing in the process.

Transmission Meditation workshops are regularly held by Benjamin Creme's co-workers and Transmission Meditation groups are growing in number worldwide.

[See Benjamin Creme, *Transmission: A Meditation for the New Age*, Share International Foundation.]

For more information or to request a referral, write to one of the three Share International offices listed at the end of this book or visit our website:

www.share-international.org/transmission

The Great Invocation

From the point of Light within the Mind of God
Let light stream forth into the minds of men.
Let Light descend on Earth.

From the point of Love within the Heart of God
Let love stream forth into the hearts of men.
May Christ return to Earth.

From the centre where the Will of God is known
Let purpose guide the little wills of men –
The purpose which the Masters know and serve.

From the centre which we call the race of men
Let the Plan of Love and Light work out
And may it seal the door where evil dwells.

Let Light and Love and Power restore
the Plan on Earth.

SHARE INTERNATIONAL MAGAZINE
ISSN 01691341

A unique magazine featuring each month: information about the emergence of Maitreya, the World Teacher; articles from a Master of Wisdom; expansions of the esoteric teachings; Benjamin Creme's transcribed answers to a wide variety of topical and esoteric questions; reports of worldwide miracles; articles by and interviews with people at the forefront of progressive world change; news from UN agencies and reports of positive developments in the transformation of our world.

Share International brings together the two major directions of New Age thinking – the political and the spiritual. It shows the synthesis underlying the political, social, economic and spiritual changes now occurring on a global scale, and seeks to stimulate practical action to rebuild our world along more just and compassionate lines.

Share International covers news, events and comments related to Maitreya's priorities: an adequate supply of the right food, housing and shelter for all, healthcare and education as universal rights, and the maintenance of ecological balance in the world.

Versions of *Share International* are available in Dutch, French, German, Japanese, Romanian, Slovenian and Spanish. For subscription information, contact the appropriate office below.

For North, Central and South America, Australia, New Zealand and the Philippines
Share International
PO Box 5668, Santa Monica CA 90409 USA
[For magazine subscription only]

For the UK
Share International
PO Box 3677, London NW5 1RU, UK

For the rest of the world
Share International
PO Box 41877, 1009 DB Amsterdam, Holland

Extensive information and excerpts from the magazine
are published online.
www.share-international.org

FURTHER READING

(Books listed in order of publication.)

The Reappearance of the Christ and the Masters of Wisdom

In his first book, Benjamin Creme gives the background and pertinent information concerning the emergence of Maitreya (the Christ), as World Teacher for the New Age now dawning. Expected under different names by all religious groups, Maitreya comes to help us create co-operation among the many ideological factions, galvanize world goodwill and sharing, and inspire sweeping political, social, economic and environmental reforms. Benjamin Creme puts the most profound event of the last 2,000 years into its correct historical and esoteric context and describes what effect the World Teacher's presence will have on both the world's institutions and the average person. Through his telepathic contact with a Master of Wisdom, Creme offers insights on such subjects as the soul and reincarnation; fear of death; telepathy; meditation; nuclear energy; ancient civilizations; UFOs; problems of the developing world; a new economic order; the antichrist; and the 'last judgement'.

1st edition 1979. 2nd edition 2007. ISBN: 978-90-71484-32-2, 288pp.

Messages from Maitreya the Christ

During the years of preparation for His emergence, Maitreya gave 140 Messages through Benjamin Creme during public lectures in London from 1977 to 1982. The method used was mental overshadowing and a telepathic rapport thus set up.

Maitreya's Messages of sharing, co-operation and unity inspire readers to spread the news of His reappearance and to work urgently for the rescue of millions suffering from poverty and starvation in a world of plenty. In Message No. 11 Maitreya says: "My Plan is to show you that the way out of your problems is to listen again to the true voice of God within your hearts, to share the produce of this most bountiful of worlds among your brothers and sisters everywhere...." (5 January 1978)

Maitreya's words are a unique source of wisdom, hope and succour at this critical time of world change, and when read aloud these profound yet simple Messages invoke His energy and blessing.

1st edition Vol. I 1981, Vol. II 1986. 2nd, combined, edition 1992, reprinted 2001. ISBN 978-90-71484-22-3, 286pp.

Transmission: A Meditation for the New Age

Transmission Meditation is a form of group meditation for the purpose of 'stepping down' (transforming) spiritual energies which thus become accessible and useful to the general public. It is the creation, in co-operation with the Hierarchy of Masters, of a vortex or pool of higher energy for the benefit of humanity.

Introduced in 1974 by Benjamin Creme, under the direction of his Master, this is a form of service which is simple to do and is at the same time a powerful means of personal growth. The meditation is a combination of two yogas: Karma Yoga (yoga of service) and Laya Yoga (yoga of energy or chakras). It is a service in which we can be involved for the rest of our lives knowing that we are helping the evolution of humanity into, and beyond, the New Age. There are hundreds of Transmission Meditation groups active in many countries around the world.

In this practical and inspiring book Benjamin Creme describes the aims, technique and results of Transmission Meditation, as well as the underlying purpose of the meditation for the development of disciples.

1st edition 1983. 5th edition 2006. ISBN 978-90-71484-35-3, 212pp.

A Master Speaks

Humanity is guided from behind the scenes by a highly evolved and illumined group of men Who have preceded us along the path of evolution. These Masters of Wisdom, as They are called, seldom appear openly, but usually work through Their disciples – men and women who influence society through their work in science, education, art, religion, politics, and in every department of life.

British artist Benjamin Creme is a disciple of a Master with Whom he is in close telepathic contact. Since the launching of Share International, the magazine of which Benjamin Creme is editor, his Master has contributed to every issue an inspiring article on a wide range of subjects: reason and intuition; the new civilization; health and healing; the art of living; the need for synthesis; justice is divine; the Son of Man; human rights; the law of rebirth; the end of hunger; sharing for peace; the rise of people power; the brightest future; co-operation – and many more.

The major purpose of these articles is to draw attention to the needs of the present and the immediate future time, and to give information about the teachings of Maitreya, the Master of all the Masters. This third edition contains all 223 articles from the first 22 volumes of Share International.

1st edition 1985. 3rd expanded edition 2004.
ISBN 978-90-71484-29-2, 452pp.

Maitreya's Mission, Volume One

The first of a trilogy of books which describe the emergence and teachings of Maitreya, the World Teacher. As human consciousness steadily matures, many of the ancient 'mysteries' are now being revealed. This volume

can be seen as a guidebook for humanity as it travels on the evolutionary journey. The book's canvas is vast: from the new teachings of the Christ to meditation and karma; from life after death, and reincarnation, to healing and social transformation; from initiation and the role of service to the Seven Rays; from Leonardo da Vinci and Mozart to Sathya Sai Baba. It sets the scene and prepares the way for the work of Maitreya, as World Teacher, and the creation of a new and better life for all. It is a powerful message of hope.
1st edition 1986. 3rd edition 1993, reprinted 2003.
ISBN 978-90-71484-08-7, 419pp.

Maitreya's Mission, Volume Two

This inspiring and heart-warming book offers new hope and guidance to a suffering world on the threshold of a Golden Age. It presents the teachings of Maitreya, the World Teacher, on both the outer, practical, and inner, spiritual levels; His uniquely accurate forecasts of world events, which have astonished international media; and His miraculous appearances which have brought hope and inspiration to many thousands. It also contains a series of unique interviews with Benjamin Creme's Master which throw new and revealing light on some of the greatest problems facing humanity.

This book covers an enormous range: Maitreya's teachings; the growth of consciousness; new forms of government; commercialization and market forces; the principal of sharing; life in the New Age; schools without walls; the Technology of Light; crop circles; the Self; telepathy; disease and death; energy and thought; Transmission Meditation; the soul's purpose. Also includes transcripts of Benjamin Creme's inspiring talks on 'The Overcoming of Fear' and 'The Call to Service'.
1st edition 1993, reprinted 2004. 2nd edition 2013. ISBN 978-94-91732-02-7, 739pp.

The Ageless Wisdom Teaching

An overview of humanity's spiritual legacy, this booklet serves as a concise and easy-to-understand introduction to the Ageless Wisdom Teaching. It explains the basic tenets of esotericism, including: source of the Teaching; the emergence of the World Teacher; rebirth and reincarnation; the Law of Cause and Effect; the Plan of evolution; origin of man; meditation and service; future changes. Also included is an esoteric glossary and a recommended reading list.

1st edition 1996, reprinted 2006. ISBN 978-90-71484-13-1, 79pp.

Maitreya's Mission, Volume Three

Benjamin Creme presents a compelling vision of the future. With Maitreya, the World Teacher, and His disciples the Masters of Wisdom openly offering Their guidance, humanity will create a civilization worthy of its divine potential. Peace will be established; sharing the world's resources the norm; maintaining our environment a top priority. The new education will teach the fact of the soul and the evolution of consciousness. The cities of the world will be transformed into centres of great beauty.

This book offers invaluable wisdom on a vast range of topics. It includes Maitreya's priorities for the future, and interviews with a Master of Wisdom on 'The Challenge of the 21st Century'. It explores karma and reincarnation, the origin of humanity, meditation and service, the Plan of evolution, and other fundamental concepts of the Ageless Wisdom Teachings. It includes a fascinating look from an esoteric, spiritual perspective at ten famous artists – among them da Vinci, Michelangelo and Rembrandt – by Benjamin Creme, himself an artist.

Like the first two volumes of *Maitreya's Mission*, this work combines profound spiritual truths with practical solutions to today's most vexing problems. It is indeed a message of hope for a humanity ready to "begin the creation of a civilization such as this world has never yet seen".

1st edition 1997, reprinted 2010. ISBN 978-90-71484-45-2, 694pp

The Great Approach: New Light and Life for Humanity

This prophetic book addresses the problems of our chaotic world and its gradual change under the influence of a group of perfected men, the Masters of Wisdom, Who, with Their leader Maitreya, the World Teacher, are returning openly to the world for the first time in 98,000 years.

The book covers such topics as: sharing; the USA in a quandary; ethnic conflicts; crime and violence; environment and pollution; genetic engineering; science and religion; the nature of light; health and healing; education; miracles; the soul and incarnation. An extraordinary synthesis of knowledge, it throws a searchlight on the future; with clear vision it predicts our highest achievements of thought to reveal the amazing scientific discoveries which lie ahead. It shows us a world in which war is a thing of the past, and the needs of all are met.

1st edition 2001. ISBN 978-90-71484-23-0, 320pp.

The Art of Co-operation

The *Art of Co-operation* deals with the most pressing problems of our time, and their solution, from the point of view of the Ageless Wisdom Teachings that, for millennia, have revealed the forces underlying the outer world. Benjamin Creme brings these teachings up to date, preparing the way for the imminent emergence of Maitreya, the World Teacher, and His group of Masters of Wisdom.

This volume looks at a world locked in ancient competition, trying to solve its problems by old and out-worn methods, while the answer – co-operation – lies in our own hands. It shows the way to a world of justice, freedom and peace through a growing appreciation of the unity underlying all life. Maitreya will inspire in us this growing realization.

Topics include: the necessity of co-operation; the USA and competition; organism versus organization; opportunity for service; fear of loss; karma; love; courage and detachment; overcoming of glamour; how the Masters teach; unity in diversity; consensus; trust.

1st edition 2002. ISBN 978-90-71484-26-1, 235pp.

Maitreya's Teachings: The Laws of Life

We do not have even fragments of the teachings of former World Teachers given prior to certain knowledge of Their existence. We do not have the teachings of a Christ, or a Buddha, or a Krishna, except seen through the eyes of later followers. For the first time we are given the flavour of the thoughts and insights of a Being of immeasurable stature to enable us to understand the path of evolution stretching ahead of us which He has come to outline for us. The impression left in the mind by the Teacher is that the breadth and depth of His knowledge and awareness have no limits; that He is tolerant and wise beyond conception, and of amazing humility.

Few could read from these pages without being changed. To some the extraordinary insights into world events will be of major interest, while to others the laying bare of the secrets of self-realization, the simple description of experienced truth, will be a revelation. To anyone seeking to understand the Laws of Life, these subtle and pregnant insights will take them quickly to the core of Life itself, and provide them with a simple path stretching to the mountain-top. The essential unity of all life is underscored in a clear and meaningful way. Never, it would appear, have the Laws by which we live seemed so natural and so unconstraining.

1st edition, 2005. ISBN 978-90-71484-31-5, 258pp.

The Art of Living: Living Within the Laws of Life
Inspired by the writings of two Masters of Wisdom – the Master Djwhal Khul and, particularly, Benjamin Creme's own Master – Part One of this book considers the experience of living as a form of art, like painting or music. To reach a high level of expression requires both knowledge of and adherence to certain fundamental principles. In the art of life, it is through the understanding of the great Law of Cause and Effect, and the related Law of Rebirth, that we achieve the poised harmlessness that leads to personal happiness, right human relations and the correct path for all humanity on its evolutionary journey.

Parts Two and Three, 'The Pairs of Opposites' and 'Illusion', propose that it is man's unique position in the evolutionary scheme – the meeting point of spirit and matter – that produces his seemingly endless struggle both within himself and in outer living. The means by which he emerges from the fog of illusion, and blends these two aspects of himself into one perfect Whole, is living life itself with growing detachment and objective self-awareness.

1st edition 2006. ISBN 978- 90-71484-37-7, 215pp.

The World Teacher for All Humanity
Maitreya, the World Teacher, stands poised, ready to emerge into full public work. This book presents an overview of this momentous event: the return to the everyday world of Maitreya in July 1977 and the gradual emergence of His group, the Masters of Wisdom; the

252

enormous changes that Maitreya's presence has brought about; and His plans, priorities and recommendations for the immediate future. It discusses in detail the quality and capacity of Maitreya based on a series of articles written by Benjamin Creme's Master – Maitreya as a great spiritual Avatar with immeasurable love, wisdom and power; and, as a friend and brother of humanity who is here to lead the whole of humanity into the New Age of Aquarius.

1st edition, 2007. ISBN 978-90-71484-39-1, 132pp.

The Awakening of Humanity

A companion volume to *The World Teacher for All Humanity*, published in 2007, which emphasizes the nature of Maitreya as World Teacher, the Embodiment of Love and Wisdom.

The *Awakening of Humanity* focuses on the day when Maitreya declares Himself openly as World Teacher for the Age of Aquarius. It describes the process of Maitreya's emergence, the steps leading to the Day of Declaration, and humanity's response to this momentous experience.

Of the Day of Declaration Benjamin Creme's Master says: "Never, before, will men have heard the call to their divinity, the challenge to their presence here on Earth. Each, singly, and solemnly alone, will know for that time the purpose and meaning of their lives, will experience anew the grace of childhood, the purity of aspiration cleansed of self. For these precious minutes, men will know afresh the joy of full participation in the realities of Life, will feel connected one to another, like the memory of a distant past."

1st edition 2008. ISBN 978-90-71484-41-4, 141pp.

The Gathering of the Forces of Light: UFOs and Their Spiritual Mission

This is a book about UFOs, but with a difference. It is written by someone who has worked with them and knows about them from the inside. Benjamin Creme sees the presence of UFOs as planned and of immense value for the people of Earth.

According to Benjamin Creme, the UFOs and the people in them are engaged on a spiritual mission to ease humanity's lot and to save this planet from further and faster destruction. Our own planetary Hierarchy, led by Maitreya, the World Teacher, now living among us, works tirelessly with their Space Brothers in a fraternal enterprise to restore sanity to this Earth.

Topics covered in this unique book include: the Space Brothers' work on Earth; George Adamski; crop circles; the new Technology of Light; Benjamin Creme's work with the Space Brothers; the dangers of nuclear radiation; saving the planet; the 'star' heralding Maitreya's emergence; Maitreya's first interview; education in the New Age; intuition and creativity; family and karma.

Part One "UFOs and Their Spiritual Mission"; Part Two "Education in the New Age".

1st edition 2010. ISBN 978-90-71484-46-9, 223pp.

Unity in Diversity: The Way Ahead for Humanity

We need a new, hopeful vision for the future. This book presents such a vision: a future that embraces a world at peace in harmony and unity, while each individual quality and approach is welcomed and needed. It is visionary, but is expressed with a cogent and compelling logic.

This book concerns the future of every man, woman and child. It is about the future of the Earth itself. Humanity, Creme says, is at a crossroads and has a major decision to make: to go onwards and create a brilliant new civilisation in which all are free and social justice reigns, or continue as we are, divided and competing, and see the end of life on planet Earth.

Creme writes for the Spiritual Hierarchy on Earth, whose Plan for the betterment of all humanity he presents. He shows that the path forward for us all is the realisation of our essential unity without the sacrifice of our equally essential diversity.

1st edition 2012. ISBN 978-90-71484-98-8, 167pp.

~ ~ ~

Benjamin Creme's books have been translated and published in Dutch, French, German, Japanese and Spanish by groups responding to this message. Some have also been published in Chinese, Croatian, Finnish, Greek, Hebrew, Italian, Portuguese, Romanian, Russian, Slovenian and Swedish. Further translations are planned. Books are available from local booksellers as well as online vendors.

Share-International.org/books
See also 'Other Languages' on this site

For the U.S.A.
Share International USA
P.O. Box 5537
Berkeley, CA 94705